INDIRECT TAX

Qualifications and Credit Framework

Level 3 Diploma in Accounting

For assessments from 1 January 2013

British Library Cataloguing-in-Publication Data

A catalogue record for this book is available from the British Library.

Published by
Kaplan Publishing UK
Unit 2, The Business Centre
Molly Millars Lane
Wokingham
Berkshire
RG41 2QZ

ISBN 978-0-85732-601-0

We are grateful to the Association of Accounting Technicians for permission to reproduce past assessment materials and example tasks based on the new syllabus. The solutions to past answers and similar activities in the style of the new syllabus have been prepared by Kaplan Publishing.

The Indirect Tax Reference material in the Appendix to this textbook has been supplied by the Association of Accounting Technicians. We are grateful for their permission to include this material in full.

We are grateful to HM Revenue and Customs for the provision of tax forms, which are Crown Copyright and are reproduced here with kind permission from the Office of Public Sector Information.

Information reproduced from the VAT Guide 700 is also subject to Crown Copyright.

CONTENTS

STUDY TEXT AND WORKBOOK

KAPLAN PUBLISHING

INTRODUCTION

HOW TO USE THESE MATERIALS

These Kaplan Publishing learning materials have been carefully designed to make your learning experience as easy as possible and to give you the best chance of success in your AAT assessments.

They contain a number of features to help you in the study process.

The sections on the Unit Guide, the Assessment and Study Skills should be read before you commence your studies.

They are designed to familiarise you with the nature and content of the assessment and to give you tips on how best to approach your studies.

STUDY TEXT

This study text has been specially prepared for the AAT qualification...

It is written in a practical and interactive style:

- key terms and concepts are clearly defined

- all topics are illustrated with practical examples with clearly worked solutions based on sample tasks provided by the AAT

- frequent activities throughout the chapters ensure that what you have learnt is regularly reinforced

- 'pitfalls' and 'examination tips' help you avoid commonly made mistakes and help you focus on what is required to perform well in your examination

- practice workbook activities can be completed at the end of each chapter.

WORKBOOK

The workbook comprises:

Practice activities at the end of each chapter with solutions at the erd of this text, to reinforce the work covered in each chapter.

Students may either attempt these questions as they work through the textbook, or leave some or all of these until they have completed the textbook as a final revision of what they have studied.

ICONS

The study chapters include the following icons throughout.

They are designed to assist you in your studies by identifying key definitions and the points at which you can test yourself on the knowledge gained.

 Definition

These sections explain important areas of Knowledge which must be understood and reproduced in an assessment

 Example

The illustrative examples can be used to help develop an understanding of topics before attempting the activity exercises

 Activity

These are exercises which give the opportunity to assess your understanding of all the assessment areas.

 Reference material

These boxes will direct you to the Official Reference Material that you can access during your real assessment. A copy of this reference material is included as an Appendix to this document.

UNIT GUIDE

Indirect tax is divided into two units but for the purposes of assessment these units will be combined.

Principles of VAT (Knowledge)

2 credits

Preparing and Completing VAT returns (Skills)

2 credits

Purpose of the units

The AAT has stated that this unit is designed to ensure that learners can understand VAT regulations, accurately complete VAT returns and communicate VAT information to relevant people.

As VAT is subject to specific and detailed regulations, the learner should be able to seek guidance from relevant sources, process what is found and communicate this to others.

Learning objectives

On completion of these units the learner will be:

- able to deal with the most commonly occurring VAT issues in a business. Although some basic knowledge will be expected, the emphasis is not so much on recall as on awareness and understanding

- aware that regulations exist and know how to find the information to ensure that the business complies with the regulations and avoids surcharges and penalties

- able to extract information from the relevant source and, using their knowledge and understanding, apply the rules to the given situations

- aware of registration requirements and the existence of a variety of schemes with different requirements to suit businesses with different needs

- able to calculate VAT correctly and use an accounting system to extract the figures required to complete the VAT return

- aware of the special circumstances that require particular attention and be able to deal with errors and changes in the VAT rate, as well as being able to communicate on VAT issues with people inside and outside the business.

Learning Outcomes and Assessment criteria

The unit consists of three learning outcomes, one for Knowledge and two for Skills, which are further broken down into Assessment criteria. These are set out in the following table with Learning Outcomes in bold type and Assessment criteria listed underneath each Learning Outcome. Reference is also made to the relevant chapter within the text.

Knowledge

To perform this unit effectively you will need to know and understand the following:

		Chapter
1	**Understand VAT regulations**	
1.1	Identify sources of information on VAT	1
1.2	Explain the relationship between the organisation and the relevant government agency	1
1.3	Explain the VAT registration requirements	2
1.4	Identify the information that must be included on business documentation of VAT registered businesses	3
1.5	Recognise different types of inputs and outputs	1, 3, 4, 7
1.6	Identify how different types of supply are classified for VAT purposes	1, 7, 8

- standard supplies

- exempt supplies

- zero rated supplies

- imports

- exports

KAPLAN PUBLISHING

Chapter

1.7	Explain the requirements and the frequency of reporting for the following VAT schemes	5

- annual accounting
- cash accounting
- flat rate scheme
- standard scheme

1.8	Recognise the implications and penalties for the organisation resulting from failure to abide by VAT regulations including the late submission of VAT returns	6

Skills

To perform this unit effectively you will need to be able to do the following.

Chapter

1 Complete VAT returns accurately and in a timely manner

1.1	Correctly identify and extract relevant data for a specific period from the accounting system	7,8
1.2	Calculate accurately relevant inputs and outputs	1, 3, 4, 7, 8

- standard supplies
- exempt supplies
- zero rated supplies
- imports
- exports

1.3	Calculate accurately the VAT due to, or from, the relevant tax authority	7, 8
1.4	Make adjustments and declarations for any errors or omissions identified in previous VAT periods	6, 7, 8
1.5	Complete accurately and submit a VAT return within the statutory time limits along with any associated payments	5, 7, 8

Delivery guidance

The AAT have provided delivery guidance giving further details of the way in which the unit will be assessed.

Principles of VAT – Understand VAT regulations

1.1   Identify sources of information on VAT

- Extract information from relevant sources.

1.2   Explain the relationship between the organisation and the relevant government authority. Understanding that:

- HMRC is a government body entitled to require organisations to comply with VAT regulations in relation to registration, record keeping, submission of returns.

- VAT is a tax on consumer expenditure.

- it is advisable to get written confirmation from HMRC about issues on which doubt may arise as to the correct treatment.

- HMRC are entitled to inspect VAT records during control visits (no further details of control visits is expected).

1.3   Explain the VAT registration requirements

- The registration threshold and when registration becomes compulsory.

- Circumstances in which voluntary registration may be beneficial to the business.

- Awareness of circumstances when deregistration may be appropriate, and the deregistration threshold.

- Which records must be kept and for how long.

KAPLAN PUBLISHING

1.4 Identify the information that must be included on business documentation of VAT registered businesses, including;

- Less detailed VAT invoices, VAT receipts, and invoicing for zero rated and exempt supplies.

- Tax points – basic and actual, including where payment is in advance of supply or invoice is after the supply, but not continuous supply or goods on sale or return. The importance of tax points for determining eligibility for schemes, correct rate of VAT, and including figures on the VAT return.

- Time limits for VAT invoices including the 14-day rule.

- Rounding rules.

- Information that is not required.

1.5 Recognise different types of inputs and outputs

- What are inputs and outputs, and what are input and output tax?

- How to treat different types of inputs and outputs in preparing a VAT return, including proforma invoices.

- The implication of the difference between zero rated and exempt supplies with respect to reclaiming input VAT should be recognised.

1.6 Identify how different types of supply are classified for VAT purposes

- standard supplies

- exempt supplies

- zero rated supplies

- imports

- exports

- No knowledge required of the detail of which specific items fall into each category.

- The basics of partial exemption, including an awareness of the de minimis limit that enables full recovery of input VAT for businesses with mixed exempt and taxable supplies. Calculations will not be required.

- Candidates will not be required to understand out of scope at this stage.

1.7 Explain the requirements and the frequency of reporting for the following VAT schemes

- annual accounting

- cash accounting

- flat-rate scheme

- standard scheme

- be able to explain in broad terms the way in which each scheme works and the situations in which an organisation would be likely to use one.

- know the effect of each scheme on the frequency of VAT reporting and payments.

1.8 Recognise the implications and penalties for the organisation resulting from failure to abide by VAT regulations including the late submission of VAT returns

The main principles of the enforcement regime, but not the fine detail.

- What triggers a surcharge liability notice. Will not be expected to know how the amount of the surcharge is calculated, or what happens if a further default arises in the surcharge period, etc.

- Penalties – awareness of fines and that evasion of VAT is a criminal offence.

Preparing and completing VAT returns

Complete VAT returns accurately and in a timely manner

1.1 Correctly identify and extract relevant data for a specific period from the accounting system

Learners will be expected to extract relevant income, expenditure and VAT figures from the accounting system

- sales day book

- purchases day book

- cash book

- petty cash book

- journal

- general ledger accounts for sales, purchases, input VAT, output VAT.

1.2 Calculate accurately relevant inputs and outputs

- Using the basic rounding rule calculate correctly the VAT and input and output figures for

- Standard supplies

- Exempt supplies

- Zero rated supplies

- Imports

- Exports

- The detailed rounding rules based on lines of goods and services and tax per unit or article are not required.

- No knowledge required of the detail of which specific items fall into each category of standard, exempt and zero rated.

- Be able to calculate VAT from net sales amounts at different rates of VAT, including cases when a settlement discount is offered.

- Be able to calculate the amount of VAT arising when given either the gross amount or the net amount of a supply.

- Know in broad terms how imports and exports, and their related VAT, are treated on a VAT return, including the significance of the EC.(Candidates are not expected to have knowledge of Intrastat returns).

- Know that exports are normally zero rated.

- Correctly account for VAT on business entertainment, sales and purchases of cars and vans and deposits or advance payments.

- Be aware of fuel scale charges and the effect on the total VAT payable/reclaimable (but no calculations).

1.3 Calculate accurately the VAT due to, or from, the relevant tax authority. In respect of:

- Transactions in the current period.

- Adjustments for bad debt relief.

1.4 Make adjustments and declarations for any errors or omissions identified in previous VAT periods

- The errors or omissions will be given.

- Identify whether the error or omission can be corrected on the current VAT return by identifying the threshold at which errors must be declared and the timescale during which corrections can be made.

- Apply the correct treatment.

- How to report an error that cannot be corrected on the current VAT return.

1.5 Complete accurately and submit a VAT return within the statutory time limits along with any associated payments

- Knowledge of what the time limits are, including those relating to non-standard schemes.

- Accurate calculation of the VAT due to, or from, HMRC, both in respect of transactions in the current period and also in relation to errors and omissions identified from previous periods.

  Transactions include sales and purchase invoices and credits, cash payments and receipts, petty cash payments.

- Complete all the relevant sections of the VAT return (and in the manner laid down by HM Revenue & Customs)

- Be aware that most businesses will need to submit the VAT return and pay online, and that the submission dates for the return and payment differ accordingly.

- Understand that the balance on the VAT control account should agree to the figure on the VAT return and provide explanations for any difference.

Communicate VAT information

2.1 Inform managers of the impact that the VAT payment may have on the company cash flow and financial forecasts

- Know the time limits within which payment must be made under various schemes.

- Communicate this via standard communication methods such as emails.

2.2 Advise relevant people of the impact that any changes in VAT legislation, including the VAT rate, would have on the organisation's recording systems

- Basic understanding of the implication of a change in the VAT rate on the organisation using either manual or computerised systems.

- Basic understanding of who would need to be informed and why.

- Advise relevant people by email or other appropriate means.

2.3 Communicate effectively with the relevant tax authority when seeking guidance

- Knowledge of the expected methods of communication.

- Able to use all forms of communication where appropriate.

THE ASSESSMENT

The format of the assessment

The assessment will be divided into two sections comprising of eight tasks.

Section 1:

There are five short-answer tasks assessing the learner's knowledge of the principles of VAT and their ability to understand and interpret VAT guidance given to them.

Some simple calculations will be required.

A number of the tasks will be multiple choice or true / false statements.

Section 2:

There will be three tasks. These will include the completion of a VAT return from information extracted from the accounting system and a short piece of communication to an internal or external person.

Learners will be required to demonstrate competence in both sections of the assessment.

The computer based assessment will be provided by AAT and delivered online.

The Official Reference Material is available to study before the assessment, via the AAT website, and in the Appendix to this study text.

It is accessed during the assessment by clicking the appropriate heading on the right hand side of the screen.

Time allowed

The time allowed for this assessment is **90 minutes.**

Pass mark

The pass mark is 70%.

STUDY SKILLS

Preparing to study

Devise a study plan

Determine which times of the week you will study.

Split these times into sessions of at least one hour for study of new material. Any shorter periods could be used for revision or practice.

Put the times you plan to study onto a study plan for the weeks from now until the assessment and set yourself targets for each period of study – in your sessions make sure you cover the whole course, activities and the associated questions in the workbook at the back of the manual.

If you are studying more than one unit at a time, try to vary your subjects as this can help to keep you interested and see subjects as part of wider knowledge.

When working through your course, compare your progress with your plan and, if necessary, re-plan your work (perhaps including extra sessions) or, if you are ahead, do some extra revision / practice questions.

Effective studying

Active reading

You are not expected to learn the text by rote, rather, you must understand what you are reading and be able to use it to pass the assessment and develop good practice.

A good technique is to use SQ3Rs – Survey, Question, Read, Recall, Review:

1   Survey the chapter

Look at the headings and read the introduction, knowledge, skills and content, so as to get an overview of what the chapter deals with.

2   Question

Whilst undertaking the survey ask yourself the questions you hope the chapter will answer for you.

3 Read

Read through the chapter thoroughly working through the activities and, at the end, making sure that you can meet the learning objectives highlighted on the first page.

4 Recall

At the end of each section and at the end of the chapter, try to recall the main ideas of the section / chapter without referring to the text. This is best done after short break of a couple of minutes after the reading stage.

5 Review

Check that your recall notes are correct.

You may also find it helpful to re-read the chapter to try and see the topic(s) it deals with as a whole.

Note taking

Taking notes is a useful way of learning, but do not simply copy out the text.

The notes must:

- be in your own words
- be concise
- cover the key points
- be well organised
- be modified as you study further chapters in this text or in related ones.

Trying to summarise a chapter without referring to the text can be a useful way of determining which areas you know and which you don't.

Three ways of taking notes

1 Summarise the key points of a chapter

2 Make linear notes

A list of headings, subdivided with sub-headings listing the key points.

If you use linear notes, you can use different colours to highlight key points and keep topic areas together.

Use plenty of space to make your notes easy to use.

3 Try a diagrammatic form

The most common of which is a mind map.

To make a mind map, put the main heading in the centre of the paper and put a circle around it.

Draw lines radiating from this to the main sub-headings which again have circles around them.

Continue the process from the sub-headings to sub-sub-headings.

Highlighting and underlining

You may find it useful to underline or highlight key points in your study text – but do be selective.

You may also wish to make notes in the margins.

Further reading

In addition to this text, you should also read the "Student section" of the "Accounting Technician" magazine every month to keep abreast of any guidance from the examiners.

VAT REFERENCE INFORMATION

Note:

This information is provided for use in this Study text. You do **not** need to memorise this information. It is all included in the Official Reference Material.

Standard rate of VAT	20%
VAT fraction (standard rated) (often simplified to 1/6)	20/120
Annual registration limit	£77,000 81,000
De-registration limit	£75,000 79,000
Cash Accounting:	
Turnover threshold to join scheme	£1,350,000
Turnover threshold to leave scheme	£1,600,000
Annual Accounting:	
Turnover threshold to join scheme	£1,350,000
Turnover threshold to leave scheme	£1,600,000
Flat rate scheme:	
Annual taxable turnover limit (excluding VAT) to join scheme	£150,000
Annual total income (including VAT) to leave scheme	£230,000

Additional information

In your assessment you are provided with Official Reference Material.

This can be accessed by clicking the appropriate heading on the right hand side of the screen.

A copy of this Official Reference Material is included in the Appendix to this textbook.

It is also available to download from the AAT website www.aat.org.uk.

It is very important that you become familiar with the content of each section of the material before you sit your assessment.

Within this text we make reference to areas of the Official Reference Material which are particularly useful.

Introduction to VAT

Introduction

This chapter introduces some of the basic ideas of value added tax (VAT), which is the only tax studied in this paper on indirect tax.

This unit requires you to have knowledge of VAT rules, to be able to prepare VAT returns and be able to communicate VAT issues to the relevant people within an organisation.

KNOWLEDGE

Identify sources of information on VAT (1.1)

Explain the relationship between the organisation and the relevant government agency (1.2)

Identify how different types of supply are classified for VAT purposes (1.6)

SKILLS

Calculate accurately relevant inputs and outputs (1.2)

Communicate effectively with the relevant tax authority when seeking guidance (2.3)

CONTENTS

1   Introduction
2   Types of supply
3   Sources of information
4   HM Revenue and Customs

1 Introduction

1.1 What is VAT?

VAT is:

- an indirect tax,

- charged on most goods and services supplied within the UK,

- borne by the final consumer, and

- collected by businesses on behalf of HM Revenue and Customs (HMRC).

VAT is an indirect tax because it is paid indirectly to traders when you buy most goods and services, rather than being collected directly by HMRC from the taxpayer as a proportion of their income or gains.

VAT is charged by **taxable persons** when they make **taxable suppl es** in the course of their business.

VAT is not generally charged on non business transactions. For example, you would not have to charge VAT if you simply sold some of your spare DVDs to a friend.

1.2 Taxable persons

 Definition

Taxable persons are businesses which are (or should be) registered for VAT.

VAT registration rules are dealt with in Chapter 2.

A person can be an individual or a legal person such as a company.

1.3 Taxable supplies

Taxable supplies or outputs are most sales made by a taxable person.

Taxable supplies can also include gifts and goods taken from the business for personal use.

1.4 Output tax

Definition

The VAT charged on sales or taxable supplies is called **output tax.**

Taxable persons charge output tax to their customers and periodically, (usually quarterly), they pay it over to HMRC.

1.5 Input tax

When a business buys goods or pays expenses (inputs), then it will also be paying VAT on those purchases or expenses.

Definition

VAT paid by a business on purchases or expenses is called **input tax.**

Registered businesses are allowed to reclaim their input tax.

They do this by deducting the input tax they have paid from the output tax which they owe, and paying over the net amount only.

If the input tax exceeds the output tax, then the balance is recoverable from HMRC.

Example

A business makes sales of £10,000 plus £2,000 of VAT. Its expenditure on purchases and expenses totals £7,000 plus £1,400 of VAT.

How much VAT is payable to HMRC?

Solution

	£
Output VAT	2,000.00
Less: Input VAT	(1,400.00)
VAT due	600.00

Activity 1

Indicate whether the following statements are true or false. Tick one box on each line.

		True	False
1	VAT is a direct tax.		
2	Jake is an AAT student working for a small accountancy practice. He advertises his bicycle for sale on the practice notice board and sells the bicycle to one of his workmates for £100. He should not charge VAT on the sale.		
3	Businesses may keep all the VAT they collect from customers.		

2 Types of supply

2.1 Classification of supplies

Supplies can be **taxable**, **exempt** or **outside the scope** of VAT.

VAT is charged on taxable supplies but not on exempt supplies or supplies outside the scope of VAT. It is therefore important to be able to correctly classify supplies in order to determine whether VAT should be charged.

Supplies outside the scope of VAT include items such as wages and dividends. They are ignored for VAT purposes and are not considered further.

2.2 Taxable supplies – rates of VAT

Taxable supplies are charged to VAT at one of three rates:

- **Zero rate**: This is a tax rate of nil. No VAT is charged but it is classed as a taxable supply. Therefore it is taken into account in deciding whether a trader should register for VAT and whether input VAT is recoverable.

- **Reduced rate**: Some supplies, mainly for domestic and charitable purposes are charged at the reduced rate.
- **Standard rate**: Any taxable supply which is not charged at the zero or reduced rates is charged at the standard rate.

Currently **the standard** rate of VAT is 20% and the reduced rate is 5%.

In order to calculate VAT on a VAT exclusive supply which is taxable at the standard rate, you multiply by 20%.

If the amount of the taxable supply is given as a VAT inclusive figure then you can find the amount of VAT included by multiplying by 20/120 (the VAT fraction). This is sometimes simplified to 1/6.

If the supply is at the reduced rate then you multiply the VAT exclusive figure by 5% and the VAT inclusive figure by 5/105 or 1/21.

These rates are summarised in the following table

Rate of VAT	% to apply to VAT exclusive amounts to calculate VAT	Fraction to apply to find VAT in VAT inclusive amounts
Standard	20%	20/120 or 1/6
Reduced	5%	5/105 or 1/21

Example

A business makes taxable sales of £12,000.

(i) What is the VAT if this is a standard rated net of VAT amount?
£12,000 × 20% = £2,400.00

(ii) What is the VAT if this is a standard rated VAT inclusive amount?
£12,000 × 20/120 = £2,000.00

(iii) What is the VAT if this is a reduced rate net of VAT amount?
£12,000 × 5% = £600.00

(iv) What is the VAT if this is a reduced rated VAT inclusive amount?
£12,000 × 5/105 = £571.42

Note that VAT is rounded down to the nearest pence (Chapter 3).

2.3   Effect of making taxable supplies

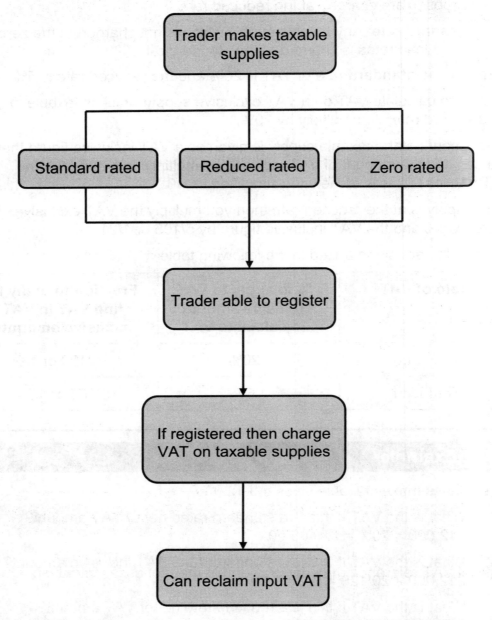

2.4   Differences between zero rated and exempt supplies

You must be careful to distinguish between traders making zero rated supplies and those making exempt supplies.

	Exempt	Zero rated
Can register for VAT?	No	Yes
Charge output VAT to customers?	No	Yes at 0%
Can recover input tax?	No	Yes

Activity 2

Select which of the word(s) in italics completes the following sentences correctly.

1   Traders making only exempt supplies …*can/must/cannot*….. register for VAT.

2   Traders who are registered for VAT must charge VAT on all their …*taxable/exempt*… supplies.

3   One of the differences between traders making zero rated supplies and traders making exempt supplies is that zero rated traders ……*can/cannot*… recover input VAT, whereas exempt traders …..*can/cannot*.

2.5   Examples of zero rated and exempt supplies

You do not need to learn lists of zero rated and exempt items. These examples are simply to show you the types of items in each category.

Zero rated	**Exempt**
Water	Rent
Most food	Insurance
Books and newspapers	Postal services
Public transport	Finance (e.g. making loans)
Children's clothes and shoes	Education (not for profit)
New house building	Betting and lotteries

 Reference material

Some information about taxable and exempt supplies is included in the official VAT reference material provided in the real assessment, so you do not need to learn it.

You need to be familiar with the location and content of the material as in the assessment you will need to access the correct part of the reference material from a series of clickable links.

Why not look up the correct part of the Official Reference Material in the Appendix to this textbook now?

3 Sources of information

3.1 Legislation

The main source of law on VAT is the VAT Act 1994 as amended by annual Finance Acts and other regulations issued by Parliament.

3.2 HMRC website

HMRC expect taxpayers to be able to answer many of their queries by searching the HMRC website at http://www.hmrc.gov.uk. Many of the HMRC publications are available to download and there a number of frequently asked questions to review.

3.3 VAT guide

HMRC issue a booklet called the **VAT Guide** Notice 700. This is the main guide to VAT rules and procedures. There are a number of supplements and amendments to the Guide to keep it up to date.

The VAT Guide is also available online on the HMRC website. As it is a large document (over 250 pages long) it is broken into sections on the website. It can be searched online or downloaded.

If you are dealing with accounting for VAT and VAT returns in practice, then you should become familiar with the contents of the VAT Guide in order to be able to refer to it when necessary.

> ### Example
>
> If you wished to look up more information about the topics covered so far in this chapter, then Section 3 of the VAT guide has the following contents.
>
> 3. General explanation of VAT: introduction and liability
>
> 3.1 Introduction to VAT
>
> 3.2 What is VAT about?
>
> 3.3 How many rates of VAT are there?
>
> 3.4 What supplies are reduced-rated?
>
> 3.5 Is VAT payable on zero-rated supplies?
>
> 3.6 Is VAT payable on exempt supplies?
>
> 3.7 Where can I find further information on liability and rates of tax?

3.4 VAT Notes

HMRC also publish a quarterly bulletin called VAT Notes. This is sent to all registered traders and contains a summary of all recent changes to the VAT rules and announces future changes.

3.5 VAT helpline

If a taxpayer cannot find the answer to their queries on the HMRC website then a telephone helpline is available. When you ring you should have a note of your VAT registration number and postcode.

Taxpayers can also email or write to HMRC with VAT queries.

 Reference material

Some information about HMRC website and the VAT helpline is included in the official VAT reference material provided in the real assessment, so you do not need to learn it.

You need to be familiar with the location and content of the material as in the assessment you will need to access the correct part of the reference material from a series of clickable links.

Why not look up the correct part of the Official Reference Material in the Appendix to this textbook now?

 HM Revenue and Customs

4.1 Introduction

As mentioned above, **HM Revenue and Customs** (HMRC) is the government body that is responsible for administering VAT.

VAT offices across the country are responsible for the local administration of VAT within a particular geographical area.

Local VAT offices deal with the collection of outstanding tax and carry out visits to taxpayers to check that they are complying with VAT rules.

HMRC are also responsible for dealing with all other issues concerning VAT including registration and record keeping (see below for record keeping requirements).

4.2 HMRC powers

HMRC have certain powers that help it administer the tax. These include:

- Inspecting premises
- Examining records
- Making assessments for underpaid tax
- Charging penalties for breaches of VAT rules (more detail on penalties can be found in Chapter 6)
- Determining whether certain supplies are liable for VAT.

4.3 Visits by VAT officers

VAT officers can visit premises to inspect records and make checks.

They normally:

- give seven days notice of a visit
- confirm in writing the details of the visit, including
  - who they wish to see
  - the date and time of the visit, and
  - the records to be inspected.

Reference material

More information about visits by VAT officers is included in the official VAT reference material provided in the real assessment, so you do not need to learn it.

You need to be familiar with the location and content of the material as in the assessment you will need to access the correct part of the reference material from a series of clickable links.

Why not look up the correct part of the Official Reference Material in the Appendix to this textbook now?

4.4 HMRC rulings

HMRC will give rulings on how they will deal with particular transactions.

This ruling is binding on HMRC provided the taxpayer has given all the necessary facts. However, it is not binding on the taxpayer who may choose to ignore the ruling, although this will almost certainly lead to a dispute with HMRC that will need to be resolved by the Tax Tribunal.

Obtaining a ruling on areas of difficulty is recommended by HMRC. This is the advice they give on their website.

"We recognise the importance for taxpayers and their advisers of being able to acquire timely and accurate advice and rulings about VAT.

Most enquiries can be dealt with by phoning our advice service. But for your own protection, you should put any major issues and more detailed questions in writing."

4.5 Communicating with HMRC

In your assessment you may be asked to draft or complete a brief piece of communication like an email or letter to HMRC to ask for information or guidance. HMRC prefer emails.

You should give the contact details and VAT registration number of the business. You may not have to complete all these details in an assessment. You should set out the nature of the query or information required.

 Example

You are Jan Smith, an AAT student who works in the accounts department of Dorn Ltd, which is a VAT registered company in Surbiton.

The company's VAT registration number is 1R3 45678.

Its telephone number is 080 456 1234.

The company manufactures widgets which it sells to large retail stores.

The company has just started to sell the widgets via mail order and you have been asked to find out how any postal charges (1% of VAT exclusive cost with a minimum charge of £2.50) should be dealt with for VAT purposes.

A suggested email would be as follows.

From   AAT student

To: HMRC

Subject: Treatment of postal charges for VAT mail order for Dorn Ltd
                VAT registration number: 1R3 45678

Dear Sir/Madam

I have a query concerning postal charges on mail order sales for Dorn Ltd.

Dorn Ltd currently manufactures widgets and sells them to retail stores. This is a standard rated business.

Mail order sales within the UK have recently started and a separate postal charge is levied.

This is 1% of the cost of widgets sold (excluding VAT), subject to a minimum charge of £2.50.

The query concerns the postal charges. I would be grateful if you could say how these should be treated for VAT.

I look forward to your reply.

Kind regards

Jan Smith

In your assessment you will only be asked to complete a short piece of communication.

Note that in practice, HMRC expect you to follow the following sequence:

- check the information publicly available in the VAT Guide 700, on their website and then
- raise the matter with the helpline
- before submitting a query.

If your query turns out to be something on which HMRC already publish information, they will reply pointing out where the information can be found.

Reference material

More information about communicating with HMRC is included in the official VAT reference material provided in the real assessment, so you do not need to learn it.

You need to be familiar with the location and content of the material as in the assessment you will need to access the correct part of the reference material from a series of clickable links.

Why not look up the correct part of the Official Reference Material in the Appendix to this textbook now?

4.6 Disputes with HMRC

Most disagreements between the taxpayer and HMRC are resolved quickly, but if an agreement cannot be reached then the taxpayer has a choice of actions.

(1) Ask for their case to be reviewed by another HMRC officer who has not previously been involved with the matter.

(2) If they do not wish the case to be reviewed by another officer, or if they disagree with the review findings, then the taxpayer can appeal to the Tax Tribunal. Such appeals are made initially to the First-tier Tax Tribunal. If the matter cannot be resolved there it may be appealed upwards to the Upper Tribunal and from there to the Court of Appeal and then the Supreme Court.

The ultimate legal authority on VAT matters is the European Court of Justice.

5 Summary

In this introductory chapter we looked at some of the basic principles and terminology used when dealing with VAT.

You should now understand that VAT is an indirect tax borne by the final consumer but collected on behalf of the government by businesses.

An important area covered in this chapter is the distinction between taxable and exempt supplies. Businesses making only exempt supplies cannot register for VAT or reclaim input tax.

If you need to find out more about VAT then it is important to know where to look. The VAT guide 700 and the HMRC website cover everything a typical business would need to know about VAT. Of course, you do not need to know all this material, you simply need to know where you might look to find it.

Communicating with HMRC is an important issue in practice. You must understand the importance of getting rulings on contentious matters in writing.

6 Test your knowledge

Workbook Activity 3

Indicate whether the following statements are true or false.

Tick one box on each line.

		True	False
1	Output tax must be charged on all sales made by a registered trader.	✓	
2	VAT is borne by the final consumer.	✓	
3	Registered traders making zero rated supplies cannot recover any input tax.		✓

Workbook Activity 4

Calculate the amount of VAT at the standard rate of 20% in respect of the following amounts. Calculate to the nearest pence.

Item	VAT inclusive amount £	VAT exclusive amount £	VAT £ p
1	472.50	78.76	55.26
2	1050	5,250.00	6300
3	846	4,230.00	5076
4	4,284.00	714	4998

Workbook Activity 5

Which one of the following is NOT a power of HMRC?

A   Inspecting premises

B   Completing your VAT return ✓

C   Examining records

D   Determining whether certain supplies are liable for VAT

 Workbook Activity 6

When a taxpayer appeals against an HMRC decision they will be offered a choice of an internal review or a referral to the Tax Tribunal.

State whether the following statement is true or false.

If a taxpayer chooses an internal review they cannot then take their case to the Tax Tribunal if they are dissatisfied with the result of the review. *Yes they can.*

 Workbook Activity 7

Which of the following is the correct definition of a taxable person?

A   A business which is registered for VAT

B   A business which should be registered for VAT

C   A business which is or should be registered for VAT ✓

D   A business which makes standard rated supplies

upon a disagreement the taxpayer would be offered an choice on the referral to the tax tribunal. If the taxpayer is not satisfied with the review made by another HMRC officer then they can appeal to Tax tribunal, first aider, if not resolved it can be brought up to the supreme tribunal.

VAT registration

Introduction

This chapter introduces the rules for both compulsory and voluntary VAT registration. It also explains when a business must deregister.

If a business does not register for VAT when it starts then a careful eye must be kept on the level of taxable turnover, (standard and zero rated supplies), to avoid missing the deadline for registration.

Remember from Chapter 1 that a taxable person is one who is, or should be, registered for VAT. This means that even if a trader does not register, they may still have a liability for VAT and they may be charged a penalty.

It is important for a business to keep the correct records both for their business and for VAT purposes. This is dealt with in this chapter.

KNOWLEDGE
Explain the VAT registration requirements (1.3)

CONTENTS
1 Compulsory registration
2 Consequences of registration
3 Voluntary registration
4 Deregistration
5 Record keeping

1 Compulsory registration

1.1 Introduction

Not all businesses need to register for VAT even if they make taxable supplies. It is only businesses that have taxable supplies exceeding the registration limits that have to register under the compulsory registration rules.

There are two separate tests for compulsory registration:

- Historic test

- Future prospects test

Note that taxable supplies for registration purposes are made up of al taxable supplies (standard, reduced and zero rated) excluding VAT and excluding the sales of capital assets. The level of exempt supplies made is not relevant in deciding whether a business has to register.

1.2 Historic test

At the end of each month, the trader must look at the cumulative total of taxable supplies for the last 12 months (or since starting in business if this is less than 12 months ago).

If the total exceeds the registration limit then the trader must register as follows:

- Notify HMRC **within 30 days** of the end of the month in which the turnover limit is exceeded.

  Notification can be made online or by post.

- Registration is effective from the **end of the month** following the month in which turnover exceeded the limit, or an agreed earlier date.

- A trader need not register if his taxable supplies for the next 12 months are expected to be less than the deregistration limit (see below).

  This helps businesses whose annual turnover is usually below the registration limit but which have experienced one particularly good year.

Reference material

Information about registration limits is included in the official VAT reference material provided in the real assessment, so you do not need to learn it.

You need to be familiar with the location and content of the material as in the assessment you will need to access the correct part of the reference material from a series of clickable links.

Why not look up the correct part of the Official Reference Material in the Appendix to this textbook now?

Example

Tariq started in business on 1 February 20X0. His taxable turnover is £10,000 per month.

He checks his taxable turnover at the end of each month and discovers at the end of September 20X0 that his taxable supplies for the previous 8 months have exceeded the registration limit.

He must notify HMRC by 30 October and will be registered with effect from 1 October or an agreed earlier date.

Activity 1

Deanna starts a business on 1 June 20X0.

Her monthly turnover of taxable supplies is £8,000.

1   Assuming the registration limit is £77,000, when does Deanna have to notify HMRC of her liability to register and from which date would she normally be registered?

2   Would your answer to (a) be any different if Deanna's turnover was made up of half standard rated and half zero rated supplies? *Yes she would.*

3   Would your answer to (a) be any different if Deanna's turnover was made up wholly of exempt supplies? *No she would need*

28 of February 20X0. she'll need to notify HMRC by email or post on that date.

1.3 Future prospects test

A liability to register will also arise if taxable supplies within the next 30 days are expected to exceed the registration limit.

This test is applied at any time, not just the end of a month, and only looks at the supplies to be made in the next 30 days in isolation.

- HMRC must be notified **before the end** of the 30 day period.

- Registration will be effective from the **beginning** of the 30 day period.

 Example

Dog Ltd signs a lease for new business premises on 1 June 20X0 and opens for business on 15 September 20X0. The company estimates that taxable supplies will be £90,000 per month starting immediately.

Assuming the registration limit is £77,000, when does Dog Ltd have to register for VAT and notify HMRC?

Solution

Dog Ltd is liable to registration because supplies for the 30 days to 14 October 20X0 are expected to exceed £77,000.

The company must notify HMRC of its liability to registration by 14 October 20X0 and is registered with effect from 15 September 20X0.

Note: Dog Ltd does not make any taxable supplies before September 20X0 so does not need to register before that date.

 Activity 2

State which of the following unregistered traders are liable to register for VAT and the effective date of registration.

Assume the registration limit is £77,000.

Name	Supplies	Details
Majid	Accountancy services	Started in business on 1 October 20X0. Estimated fees of £16,000 per month.
Jane	Baby wear	Established the business on 1 July 20X0 when Jane signed a contract to supply a local nursery. Sales for July 20X0 are expected to be £100,000.
Sayso Ltd	Insurance broker	Commenced trading 2 August 20X0 with expected sales of £100,000 per month. Insurance broking is an exempt activity.

1.4 Number of registrations

A person can be registered only once, and this registration includes all the businesses that person carries on.

Where a partnership is concerned, a separate registration is required for the partnership. Other unincorporated businesses carried on by the individual partners will have a separate single registration.

Companies are all registered individually although it is possible for companies in certain sorts of groups to have a single registration. You do not need to know any details of this.

Example

Jason is a sole trader. He owns a clothing shop "Jason's Style" which is open during the day, and in the evenings he runs a business organising parties. Both businesses have turnover of £40,000 each.

Jason is also a partner in Bash and Co, an import/export business he helps run with his wife. The partnership business has a turnover of £110,000.

Jason is also a shareholder in Xenon Ltd, a company specialising in manufacturing electronic equipment. The company has a turnover of £250,000.

Assuming the entire turnover of all of the businesses consists of taxable supplies, how many VAT registrations are required to cover these businesses? Assume the registration limit is £77,000.

Solution

There are three registrations needed here:

(a) One registration is needed to cover Jason's two sole trader businesses. Even though each business has turnover below the registration limit, the combined turnover of the businesses is over the limit.

(b) One registration will cover Bash and Co.

(c) The third registration will be needed to cover Xenon Ltd.

1.5 Exemption from registration

A trader making only zero rated supplies can apply for exemption from registration.

However, this would mean they cannot recover their input tax, and so the exemption is only likely to be applied for if:

- the trader does not want the administrative burden of complying with VAT regulations, or

- they do not have much input tax to recover.

2 Consequences of registration

2.1 Accounting for VAT

Once registered, a taxable person must start accounting for VAT.

- Output tax must be charged on taxable supplies.

- Each registered trader is allocated a VAT registration number, which must be quoted on all invoices.

- Each registered trader is allocated a tax period for filing returns, which is normally every three months and usually fits in with their accounting year end.

- Input tax on most business purchases and expenses can be recovered. (Some exceptions are dealt with in Chapter 4.) This can also include certain input VAT incurred before registration.

- Appropriate VAT records must be kept (see section 5 below).

Traders will be sent a certificate of registration which contains their registration number and is their proof of registration.

2.2 Failure to register

A trader might think they could avoid VAT by not registering. However if a trader does not register when they go over the compulsory registration limit then there are two consequences.

(i) All the VAT that the trader **should have charged** from the date they **should have registered** is payable to HMRC.

As the trader cannot now go back to their customers and charge them the VAT, they will have to pay over the VAT out of their own profits.

(ii) A penalty can be charged which is a percentage of the VAT due.

Example

Beverley runs a business manufacturing silicon cookware which is a standard rated supply. She has failed to register for VAT.

On ⁻ October 20X0 she discovers she should have been registered since 1 March 20X0. Her turnover since that date is £27,000. — *VAT included*

Beverley will have to pay over VAT of £4,500 (20/120 × £27,000) less any input tax she has suffered in this period.

3 Voluntary registration

3.1 Actual or intending traders

Even if they are not required to register, a person can register provided they are **making or intending to make taxable supplies**.

HMRC will register the trader from the date of the request for voluntary registration, or a mutually agreed earlier date.

Remember that a trader who only makes exempt supplies cannot register.

3.2 Advantages and disadvantages of voluntary registration

Advantages	Disadvantages
Avoids penalties for late registration.	Business will have to comply with the VAT administration rules which may take time away from running the business.
Can recover input VAT on purchases and expenses.	Business must charge VAT. This makes their goods more expensive than an unregistered trader selling the same items or services. This extra cost cannot be recovered by unregistered customers such as the general public.
Can disguise the small size of the business.	

4 Deregistration

4.1 Compulsory deregistration

A person must deregister when he ceases to make taxable supplies.

- HMRC should be notified within 30 days of ceasing to make taxable supplies.
- VAT registration is cancelled from the date of cessation or a mutually agreed later date.

4.2 Voluntary deregistration

A person may voluntarily deregister, even if the business continues, if there is evidence that taxable supplies in the next 12 months will not exceed the deregistration limit.

The deregistration limit is always slightly lower than the registration limit.

- The 12 month period can start at any time. It does not have to be the beginning or end of a month.
- The trader must prove to HMRC that they qualify.
- VAT registration is cancelled from the date of the request or an agreed later date.

4.3 Effect of deregistration

On deregistration, VAT output tax must be paid over on the value of capital assets and stock owned at the date of deregistration.

This takes back the input tax relief that the business would have had when it bought those assets or stock.

 Activity 3

(a) Jig Ltd closed down its business on 10 October 20X0.

. State when Jig Ltd should notify HMRC of the business cessation and from when the business will be deregistered.

(b) At 1 May 20X0, Eli thinks that his taxable turnover for the year to 30 April 20X1 will be below the deregistration limit. He immediately applies for deregistration.

State when Eli will be deregistered.

Reference material

Information about deregistration limits is included in the official VAT reference material provided in the real assessment, so you do not need to learn it.

You need to be familiar with the location and content of the material as in the assessment you will need to access the correct part of the reference material from a series of clickable links.

Why not look up the correct part of the Official Reference Material in the Appendix to this textbook now?

5 Record keeping

5.1 General requirements

Businesses must keep information which will allow the business to calculate VAT correctly and allow HMRC to check VAT returns adequately.

Generally, the business must keep records of:

- all taxable and exempt supplies made in the course of business

- all taxable supplies received in the course of business

- a summary of the total output tax and input tax for each tax period – the VAT account (see Chapter 7).

Failure to keep records can lead to a penalty.

The business must keep records to prove the figures shown on the VAT returns for the previous **six** years, although HMRC can reduce this period where the records are bulky and the information they contain can be provided in another way.

5.2 Business records

Records need to be kept for business purposes and for VAT purposes.

Business records that should be kept are:

- annual accounts including income statements (profit and loss accounts)

- bank statements, paying-in slips and cheque stubs

- cash books and other account books
- orders and delivery notes
- purchases and sales books
- recordings of daily takings, including till rolls
- relevant business correspondence.

5.3 VAT records

VAT records are needed to allow the calculation of amounts owed to HMRC or due from HMRC in each VAT period.

Records do not have to be kept in any particular way. However it must be possible for HMRC to check the records and see how the figures in your VAT return have been calculated.

Records that should be kept include:

- records of all the standard rated, reduced rate, zero rated and exempt goods and services that you buy or sell
- purchase invoices and copy sales invoices (see Chapter 3)
- any credit or debit notes issued or received (see Chapter 3)
- records of goods and services bought for which you cannot reclaim VAT
- import and export documents
- any adjustments or corrections to your VAT account or VAT invoices
- A VAT account.

Reference material

This information is included in the official VAT reference material provided in the real assessment, so you do not need to learn it.

You need to be familiar with the location and content of the material as in the assessment you will need to access the correct part of the reference material from a series of clickable links.

Why not look up the correct part of the Official Reference Material in the Appendix to this textbook now?

Registered businesses may be visited by a VAT officer on occasion to ensure that their records are being correctly maintained.

5.4 Electronic and paper VAT records

As long as the VAT records meet the requirements laid down by HMRC, they can be kept in whatever format – paper and/or electronic – that the business prefers.

Where a business keeps all or part of its records on a computer, it must make sure that the records are easily accessible if a VAT officer visits.

Records can be kept on microfilm provided HMRC have given approval and the records can be inspected when necessary.

Some businesses send or receive invoices by electronic means. This does not require approval from HMRC.

6 Summary

In this chapter we have considered which traders need to become VAT registered and the effects of registration.

Both the historic and future prospects test for registration have been set out. Remember that it is the turnover of taxable supplies, including zero rated supplies, that determines whether a business needs to register for VAT.

It is also important to remember that businesses which **only** make **exempt** supplies **cannot** register for VAT whilst businesses that **only** make **zero rated** supplies **need not** register for VAT if they do not wish to do so.

Failure to register when taxable supplies have exceeded the limit can cost a business a great deal.

Firstly they must pay over the VAT they should have collected from customers and secondly they may be charged a penalty.

Traders can choose to register voluntarily provided they are making taxable supplies now or intend to in the future. This allows the business to recover input tax, but may make the price of their goods comparatively more expensive than those of an unregistered trader

We saw that a business **must** deregister if it ceases to make taxable supplies, and **may** deregister if its taxable supplies for the next 12 months will be below the deregistration limit.

Finally the records that must be kept by a registered business were discussed.

7 Test your knowledge

 Workbook Activity 4

You are given the following information about the taxable supplies of four businesses.

Assuming that the registration limit is £77,000, for each of the businesses select whether they need to register for VAT immediately, or monitor turnover and register later.

Tick one box on each line.

		Register now	Monitor and register later
1	A new business with an expected turnover of £80,000 per month for the next 12 months.		
2	An existing business with a total turnover of £69,000 since it began trading 11 months ago. The turnover for the next month is not known.		
3	An existing business with a turnover of £6,500 per month for the last 12 months.		
4	An existing business with a turnover of £6,000 per month since it began trading six months ago which is expected to increase to £7,000 per month for the next six months.		

 Workbook Activity 5

Wayne runs three sole trader businesses and is also in partnership with his wife running a fourth business. Each of the businesses has taxable supplies exceeding the VAT registration limit.

How many VAT registrations are required?

A   1

B   2

C   3

D   4

 Workbook Activity 6

You are given the following information about four traders.

Assuming that the registration limit is £77,000 and the deregistration limit is £75,000, do the traders **have** to register for VAT?

Tick one box on each line.

		Yes	No
1	A trader making only zero rated supplies of £100,000 per year.	✓	
2	A trader who has taxable supplies of £80,000 for the last 12 months, but who expects to make only £60,000 of supplies in the next 12 months.		✓
3	A trader who runs two separate businesses making standard rated supplies of £50,000 each.	✓	
4	A trader who runs two separate businesses making standard rated supplies of £60,000 in one business and exempt supplies of £20,000 in the other.		✓

Workbook Activity 7

Assuming that the registration limit is £77,000, indicate whether the following statements are true or false.

Tick one box on each line.

		True	False
1	An unregistered trader can never have a VAT liability to HMRC.		
2	A trader making only taxable supplies of £50,000 per year cannot register for VAT.		
3	A trader making only exempt supplies of £100,000 per annum must register for VAT.		
4	A trader's VAT registration number must be quoted on all of their invoices.		
5	A registered trader must deregister if their supplies fall below the deregistration limit.		

KAPLAN PUBLISHING

Workbook Activity 8

Brown commenced in business on 1 Jan 20X1 making only taxable supplies. His turnover was as follows:

First 6 months to 30.6.20X1   £5,000 per month   30,000   72000

Next 12 months to 30.6.20X2   7 months   £7,000 per month

1   On which of the following dates does Brown exceed the registration limit of £77,000?

     A   31 December 20X1

     B   31 January 20X2

     C   28 February 20X2

     D   31 March 20X2

2   Select the date by which Brown should notify HMRC that he has exceeded the registration limit.

     A   30 January 20X2

     B   2 March 20X2

     C   30 March 20X2

     D   30 April 20X2

 Workbook Activity 9

Which one of the following is a valid reason for a business making taxable supplies to choose to register voluntarily.

A   Preparation of VAT returns would be optional

B   The business would be able to reclaim input VAT

C   It would make their prices cheaper to the general public

D   It would make their prices cheaper to VAT registered customers

VAT documentation

Introduction

This chapter looks at how VAT is collected via a VAT invoice and all the details that are required to be shown on such an invoice. Other documents such as credit notes and proforma invoices are also covered.

The rules for determining the tax point are also covered. The tax point is the date which determines in which VAT period the VAT on transactions should be included.

Finally, the importance of keeping staff up to date on changes in VAT legislation is discussed.

KNOWLEDGE

Identify the information that must be included on business documentation of VAT registered businesses (1.4)

Recognise different types of inputs and outputs (1.5)

SKILLS

Calculate accurately relevant inputs and outputs (1.2)

Advise relevant people of the impact that any changes in VAT legislation, including the VAT rate, would have on the organisation's recording systems (2.2)

CONTENTS

1   Tax point (time of supply)
2   VAT invoices
3   Other documentation
4   Changes in VAT legislation

1 Tax point (time of supply)

1.1 Introduction

 Definition

The **tax point** is the date on which the liability for output tax arises – it is the date on which a supply is recorded as taking place for the purposes of the tax return. It is also referred to as the time of supply.

Most taxable persons make a VAT return each quarter. The return must include all supplies whose tax points fall within that quarter.

1.2 The basic tax point

The **basic tax point** for goods is the date when goods are 'removed' which usually means the date of delivery of those goods or the date the customer takes the goods away.

A tax point also occurs if goods are not 'removed' but are made available to a customer – for example if a specialist installer is constructing a new machine for a customer on site in their factory, the tax point will occur when the machine is handed over and not when all the materials are delivered to the site.

For services, the tax point is the date the services are performed or completed.

 Example

Queue Ltd received an order for goods from a customer on 14 March. The goods were despatched on 18 March and the customer paid on 15 April when they received their invoice dated 13 April.

State the basic tax point date.

Solution

The tax point is 18 March, i.e. the date of despatch.

1.3 Actual tax point

The basic tax point is amended in two situations.

Earlier tax point	Later tax point
• A tax invoice is issued or a payment is received before the basic tax point	• A tax invoice is issued within 14 days after the basic tax point (14 day rule)
• In these circumstances the date of invoice or payment is the time when the supply is treated as taking place	• In these circumstances the date of issue of the invoice is the time when the supply is treated as taking place

Provided that written approval is received from the local VAT office, the 14 day rule can be varied.

For example, it can be extended to accommodate a supplier who issues all of his invoices each month on the last day of the month and would like the month end invoice date to be the tax point date.

 Reference material

Information on tax points is included in the official VAT reference material provided in the real assessment, so you do not need to learn it.

You need to be familiar with the location and content of the material as in the assessment you will need to access the correct part of the reference material from a series of clickable links.

Why not look up the correct part of the Official Reference Material in the Appendix to this textbook now?

Note that the 14 day rule cannot apply to invoices which are only for zero rated goods as these are not tax invoices.

Most exports are zero rated (see Chapter 8 for more details), so the tax point for these goods is always the earlier of the supply of goods and the receipt of payment.

1.4 Deposits received in advance

If a business receives a deposit or part payment in advance then this creates a tax point when the deposit is received. However, this is only for the deposit, not the whole supply. The business must account for the VAT included in the deposit.

No tax point is created for a returnable deposit, e.g. a deposit required to ensure the safe return of a hired item, where the deposit will be returned to the customer when they bring the item back safely.

Example

Ahmed receives a £60 deposit from a customer on 1 July. The total cost of the item is £210 including VAT at 20% and the customer pays the balance of £150 on 12 September when they collect the goods.

On 15 September Ahmed issues an invoice to his customer which he marks as paid in full.

How is VAT accounted for on this transaction?

Solution

The deposit of £60 creates a tax point on 1 July.

The amount of VAT is £10 (£60 × 20/120) and this must be entered in the VAT return which includes 1 July.

When the goods are collected and paid for on 12 September this creates a further tax point. The VAT is £25 (£150 × 20/120) and this must be included in the VAT return which includes 12 September.

 Activity 1

In each of the following cases, state the tax point date.

			Tax point
1	Goods delivered to a customer on 10 July, invoice sent out on 15 July and payment received 30 July.		15 July
2	Invoice sent out to a customer on 12 August, goods delivered to the customer on 16 August, payment received 20 September.		12 August
3	Payment received from customer on 4 September, goods sent to customer on 5 September with an invoice dated on that day.		4 September
4	Goods delivered to a customer on 13 September, invoice sent out on 30 September and payment received 31 October.		13 Sep ✓

(handwritten: "15 days", "after 14 days", "if good got deliver")

2 VAT invoices

2.1 Introduction

All businesses that are registered for VAT must provide evidence to VAT registered customers of the VAT they have been charged.

In order to do this the supplier must give or send to the purchaser a VAT invoice **within 30 days** of the earlier of:

- supply of the goods or services or
- receipt of the payment.

VAT invoices are not required:

- if the purchaser is not VAT registered or
- if the supply is wholly zero rated.

In practice it is impossible to tell if a purchaser is VAT registered or not, so traders normally issue a VAT invoice anyway.

If they are retailers selling to the public they have special rules (see below).

Similarly, traders will normally issue invoices for zero rated sales which show the same details as for other supplies, but technically this is not a VAT invoice.

The original VAT invoice is sent to the customer and forms their evidence for reclaiming input VAT. A copy must be kept by the supplier to support the calculation of output VAT.

2.2 Form of a VAT invoice

There is **no standard format for invoices**. The exact design is the choice of the business, but it must show the following details (unless the invoice is a **less detailed tax invoice** that you will see later):

- identifying number which must follow a sequence (if an invoice is spoilt or cancelled it must be kept as a VAT officer may wish to inspect it)
- date of supply (tax point) and the date of issue of the invoice
- supplier's name and address and registration number
- name and address of customer, i.e. the person to whom the goods or services are supplied

- type of supply
  - sale
  - hire purchase, credit sale, conditional sale or similar transaction
  - loan
  - exchange
  - hire, lease or rental
  - process (making goods using the customer's own materials)
  - sale on commission (e.g. an estate agent)
  - supply on sale or return
- description of the goods or services
- quantity of goods or extent of services
- rate of tax and amount payable (in sterling) excluding VAT for each separate description
- total amount payable (excluding VAT) in sterling
- rate of any cash discount offered (these are also called settlement discounts)
- separate rate and amount of VAT charged for each rate of VAT
- total amount of VAT chargeable.

A VAT invoice does NOT have to include any other items such as:

- customer's order number
- date of order
- customer's VAT registration number
- method of delivery.

📋 Reference material

This invoice contents information is included in the official VAT reference material provided in the real assessment, so you do not need to learn it.

You need to be familiar with the location and content of the material as in the assessment you will need to access the correct part of the reference material from a series of clickable links.

Why not look up the correct part of the Official Reference Material in the Appendix to this textbook now?

2.3 VAT and discounts

If a **trade discount** is given then this is deducted before VAT is calculated.

If a **settlement discount** is offered, then the VAT is always calculated as if the customer takes the maximum discount.

 Example

Joachim is in business manufacturing angle brackets which he sells to retailers.

He offers a 5% discount if goods are paid for within 10 days and a 2% discount if goods are paid for within 21 days.

He sells angle brackets with a pre-discount price of £1,000 to Kim Ltd.

How much VAT should he charge on the invoice assuming that the rate of VAT is 20%?

Solution

VAT should be calculated on the lowest amount a customer could pay. It does not matter whether the customer takes the discount or not. Accordingly, the VAT is £190 (£1,000 × 95% × 20%).

 Activity 2

An invoice is issued for standard rated goods with a list price of £380.00 (excluding VAT).

A 10% trade discount is given and a 4% settlement or cash discount is offered.

How much VAT at the standard rate of 20% should be included on the invoice?

A   £76.00

B   £65.66

C   £68.40

D   £72.96

Sometimes a business will offer to pay a customer's VAT. This is really just another form of discount.

Example

XY Ltd sells beds with a normal retail price of £240 (including VAT at 20% of £40). They run a promotional offer to pay the customers' VAT for them and hence the customer pays £200.

XY Ltd must treat the £200 paid as a VAT inclusive price and account for VAT of £33.33 (£200 × 1/6).

2.4 Example of a VAT invoice

Example

MICRO TRAINING GROUP LTD
Unit 34, Castlewell Trading Estate
Manchester M12 5RHF

To: Slough Labels Ltd	Sales invoice number:	35
Station Unit	VAT registration number:	234 5566 87
Slough	Date of issue:	30 September 20X0
SL1 3EJ	Tax point:	12 September 20X0

Sales:

No.	Description and price	Amount excl VAT £ p	VAT rate	VAT £ p
6	Programmable calculators FR34 at £24.76	148.56	20%	
12	Programmable calculators GT60 at £36.80	441.60	20%	
		590.16		115.67
	Delivery	23.45	20%	4.69
		613.61		120.36
VAT		120.36		
TOTAL		733.97		

Terms: Net 30 days.
Cash discount of 2% on goods if paid within 10 days

Note that on this invoice the VAT is calculated after applying the discount of 2% to the **goods** element of the invoice as the discount is not given on the delivery charge.

2.5 Rounding VAT

Usually, the amount of VAT calculated will not be a whole number of pounds and pence. You will therefore need a rounding adjustment.

The rules governing this adjustment are quite tricky, and permit more than one method.

However, for assessment purposes you only need to know the basic rounding rule – that is that the total amount of VAT payable on an invoice can be rounded down to the nearest penny.

 Activity 3

Calculate the total VAT to be charged in respect of each of the three VAT invoices below.

Invoice	Description and price	Net of VAT £ p	VAT rate	VAT £ p
1	16 × 6 metre hosepipes @ £3.23 each	51.68	20%	
2	24 × bags of compost @ £5.78 each	138.72	20%	
3	Supply of kitchen units	1,084.57	20%	

2.6 Less detailed (simplified) VAT invoices

Retailers (selling to the public), do not have to issue a detailed VAT invoice every time they make a sale as this would make trading in a busy shop very difficult.

If the total amount of the supply **(including VAT)** by the retailer does not exceed £250, then **when a customer requests a tax invoice** a retailer may issue a **less detailed tax invoice**. However, if requested by a customer a full VAT invoice must be issued.

The details required on the less detailed invoice are:

- supplier's name and address
- supplier's VAT registration number
- date of supply (tax point)
- description sufficient to identify the goods or services
- amount payable (including VAT) for each rate (standard and zero)
- the VAT rate applicable.

The main differences between the less detailed invoice and the full invoice are that the customer's name and address can be omitted, and the total on the invoice includes the VAT without the VAT itself being shown separately.

Although this invoice shows less detail, it is still a valid tax invoice. This means that if the purchaser is a VAT registered business they can use the invoice to support a claim for input VAT.

 Example

Delta Office Supplies

46, Central Mall, Glastonbury, Somerset
G34 7QT
Telephone: 01392 43215
15 April 20X0

1 box of 50 blank DVD-R
Total including VAT @ 20%   £25.85

VAT registration number: 653 7612 44

If the business accepts credit cards they can use the sales voucher given to the cardholder as a less detailed invoice.

However, it must still contain the details above.

Exempt supplies must not be included in a less detailed invoice.

 Reference material

Information about VAT invoices is included in the official VAT reference material provided in the real assessment, so you do not need to learn it.

You need to be familiar with the location and content of the material as in the assessment you will need to access the correct part of the reference material from a series of clickable links.

Why not look up the correct part of the Official Reference Material in the Appendix to this textbook now?

Retailers **do not have to keep** copies of the less detailed VAT invoices that they issue, whereas non retailers must keep copies of all sales invoices issued.

This is because retailers generally calculate their VAT from their **daily gross takings** rather than from individual invoices.

3 Other documentation

3.1 Credit notes

When customers return goods which were taxable supplies, the supplier may issue a credit note. This has to have similar information to that found on the original invoice and must be **clearly labelled as a credit note**.

The number and date of the original tax invoice should also appear on the credit note.

If the supplier issues the credit note without making a VAT adjustment, the credit note must say '**This is not a credit note for VAT**'.

A supplier is not allowed to issue a credit note to recover VAT on bad debts

From the supplier's point of view the VAT on the credit note issued must be deducted from output VAT payable.

From the customer's point of view the VAT on the credit note received must be deducted from input tax recoverable.

Alternatively the supplier can cancel the original invoice and reissue it with the correct figures.

3.2 Debit notes

If a customer returns goods to their supplier they can wait for the supplier to issue them with a credit note or they can issue a debit note to their supplier.

Note that these are alternatives – you cannot account for both a debit note issued and a credit note received for the same supply.

From the supplier's point of view the VAT on a debit note received from a customer must be deducted from output tax payable.

From the customer's point of view the VAT on a debit note issued must be deducted from their input tax recoverable.

The treatment of the VAT can be summarised as follows:

	SELLER (supplier)	BUYER (customer)
Seller issues credit note	Deduct from output tax	Deduct from input tax
Buyer issues debit note	Deduct from output tax	Deduct from input tax
Effect	Reduce VAT payable	Increase VAT payable

 Activity 4

A business issues a purchase debit note.
What is the effect on their VAT?

A   Output VAT will increase

B   Output VAT will decrease

C   Input VAT will increase

D   Input VAT will decrease

 Reference material

Information about debit and credit notes is included in the official VAT reference material provided in the real assessment, so you do not need to learn it.

You need to be familiar with the location and content of the material as in the assessment you will need to access the correct part of the reference material from a series of clickable links.

Why not look up the correct part of the Official Reference Material in the Appendix to this textbook now?

3.3   Proforma invoices

When a business issues a sales invoice that includes VAT, the VAT becomes payable to HMRC next time the business submits a return.

This can cause cashflow problems if the customer has not yet paid the invoice, because the business then has to pay over the VAT before collecting it from their customers.

To avoid this, a business may issue a **proforma invoice** which essentially is a demand for payment. Once payment is received, the business will then issue a 'live' invoice to replace the proforma.

Because a proforma invoice does not rank as a VAT invoice the supplier is not required to pay VAT to HMRC until the 'live' invoice is issued. For this reason, the customer cannot reclaim VAT on a proforma invoice but must instead wait until the valid VAT invoice is received.

Proforma invoices must be clearly marked with the words '**This is not a VAT invoice**'.

Reference material

Information about proforma invoices is included in the official VAT reference material provided in the real assessment, so you do not need to learn it.

You need to be familiar with the location and content of the material as in the assessment you will need to access the correct part of the reference material from a series of clickable links.

Why not look up the correct part of the Official Reference Material in the Appendix to this textbook now?

3.4   Statements and demands for payment

It is important to appreciate that only VAT invoices and credit notes should be entered in the VAT records.

When a business sends out a demand for payment or a statement there is no VAT implication.

VAT has already been recorded and the demand or statement is simply the business trying to collect what it is owed.

3.5   Orders and delivery notes

These are also ignored for VAT and cannot be used by a customer as evidence for reclaiming VAT on their purchases.

3.6   VAT only invoices

Sometimes a business needs to increase VAT charged on an earlier invoice or may have forgotten to include VAT. One solution would be to credit the original invoice and then re-invoice it. Alternatively the business can issue an invoice just for the VAT and label it as a VAT only invoice.

Such an invoice must be entered in the VAT records and the tax paid over to HMRC as usual. A registered purchaser who receives the invoice will treat it as a normal VAT invoice and be able to recover the VAT charged.

4 Changes in VAT legislation

4.1 Change in the rate of VAT

The tax point date becomes very important when there is a change in the rate of VAT or if a supply is reclassified from one rate of VAT to another. Tax invoices with a tax point date before the change must use the old rate of VAT. If they have a date on/after the change then they must use the new rate.

In the assessment you may be required to calculate VAT from net sales amounts at different rates of VAT, including cases where settlement discounts are offered.

4.2 Effect of a VAT rate change on a business

A change in the rate of VAT has a major effect on the business accounting system including the following:

- Sales invoices need to be produced with the correct rate of VAT.

- Sales prices used in quotes or for pricing invoices must include the correct rate of VAT.

- Retail businesses need to make sure that prices displayed to the public are correct.

- Staff expense claims must reclaim the correct rate of VAT on (for example) mileage expenses.

- The correct input tax reclaim must be made for purchases and expenses. Input VAT claimed should be whatever figure is shown on the invoice for the purchase or expense. However, staff would need to know the details of any rate change so that they can query any actual errors with suppliers.

Whether or not a change in VAT rate is passed on to the customer is a commercial decision for a business to make. The current prices can be maintained and the cost of a VAT increase (or profit from a VAT decrease) can be absorbed by the business.

In a manual system it is important that all relevant staff is notified of the change and its impact and that price lists are updated.

In a computerised system the accounting software must be updated to produce sales invoices at the correct rate and to deal with differing rates of VAT on purchase invoices. If the VAT is calculated at the point of sale by the till system, the system must be adjusted to take account of the new rate.

In both cases it is important that the change takes place at the correct time. For example, new prices would need to be quoted to customers from the date of change. However, sales invoices must use the rate of VAT relevant to the tax point date and not necessarily the date the invoice is raised.

4.3 Informing staff

A number of different staff within a business would need to be told about a rate change and its effects.

- IT department staff – to ensure the relevant changes are made to the computerised accounting system.

- Sales ledger staff – to raise or check sales invoices correctly.

- Purchase ledger staff – so that they can check purchase invoices correctly.

- Sales staff – to ensure customers are given correct prices.

- Marketing department staff – so that any new brochures or publicity material is correct.

- Staff generally – to ensure their expense claims are made correctly.

In your assessment you may have to complete a simple email advising relevant people of the change, as shown in the following hypothetical example.

 Example

To   Sales ledger staff
From: Junior Accountant
Subject: Change in the rate of VAT
Date: 14/3/20X0

Please note that the standard rate of VAT which applies to all our products will change on 1 April 20X0 from 20% to 22%.

Any invoices with a tax point of 1 April or later must have the new VAT rate applied.

It s important that invoices with a tax point before 1 April continue to include VAT at the old rate.

---

5 Summary

This chapter has covered two important areas for VAT – invoicing and tax points.

The tax point for a supply of goods is important as this determines the VAT period in which the VAT on those goods is included. The basic tax point is the date on which goods are delivered or collected by a customer but there are also situations in which the tax point can be earlier or later. These rules must be understood.

VAT invoices must include certain details and in normal circumstances must be given or sent to a VAT registered purchaser. In practice this means that all purchasers will be provided with a VAT invoice whether they are registered or not. However retailers are allowed to issue less detailed or modified invoices. Credit notes sent out by a business must include the same details as the invoice.

Proforma invoices must not include VAT.

Changes in the rate of VAT have a major impact on a business' recording system and you should have a basic understanding of this.

6 Test your knowledge

Workbook Activity 5

Indicate whether the following statements are true or false.

Tick one box on each line

		True	False
1	Traders do not have to supply a VAT invoice unless their customer is VAT registered.	✓	
2	Retailers can issue less detailed VAT invoices if the total amount of the supply, excluding VAT, does not exceed £250.		
3	The VAT invoice is used by a customer as their evidence for reclaiming input VAT.	✓	
4	A VAT invoice must be issued to a customer within 30 days of the tax point.	✓	

Workbook Activity 6

Calculate the amount of output VAT at the standard rate of 20% that should be charged on the following invoices.

Goods pre discount price £	Trade discount	Settlement discount	Output tax £ p
1,000	10%	2% ~~882~~	176.40
2,000	Nil	5% if paid within 7 days. 2% if paid within 21 days	380
750	8%	None	138

Workbook Activity 7

Look at the following list of items.

Select by entering the appropriate number whether the items:

1   Should only be shown on a normal detailed VAT invoice; or

2   Should be shown on both a normal detailed VAT invoice and on a less detailed invoice; or

3   Should not be shown on either form of invoice.

	Item	Number (1, 2, or 3)
A	Identifying number	1
B	Tax point date	2
C	Delivery date	3
D	Total amount of VAT payable	2
E	Customer's registration number	2

Workbook Activity 8

Which of the following statements about proforma invoices are FALSE?

Enter a tick in the final box for each false statement.

		False
A	A proforma invoice IS a valid tax invoice	✓
B	A proforma invoice IS NOT a valid tax invoice	
C	A customer receiving a proforma invoice can use it to reclaim the input tax shown	✓
D	A proforma invoice is really just a demand for payment	

 Workbook Activity 9

A business issues a sales credit note.

What is the effect on output VAT?

A   Output VAT will increase

B   Output VAT will decrease

C   Input VAT will increase

D   Input VAT will decrease

Workbook Activity 10

In each of the following cases, state the tax point date.

		Tax point
1	Goods delivered to a customer on 15 August, invoice sent out on 20 August and payment received 30 August.	
2	Proforma invoice issued 3 June, payment received 10 June, goods delivered 30 June with a tax invoice dated on that day.	
3	Goods delivered to a customer on 4 March, invoice sent out on 25 March and payment received 15 April.	
4	Invoice sent to a customer on 10 December, goods delivered 18 December and payment received 27 December.	

Workbook Activity 11

A VAT registered business receives a £100 non refundable deposit on 19 October from a customer for the supply of goods which are despatched on 25 October.

The goods are invoiced on 31 October and the balance of £350 is paid on 10 November.

Both amounts are VAT inclusive.

1 What is the tax point for the deposit?

    A   19 October

    B   25 October

    C   31 October

    D   10 November

2 What is the output VAT on the deposit?

    A   £20.00

    B   £16.66

3 What is the tax point for the balance?

    A   19 October

    B   25 October

    C   31 October

    D   10 November

4 What is the output VAT on the balance?

    A   £70.00

    B   £58.33

Workbook Activity 12

Refer to the three invoices set out below which have been received from suppliers during March 20X8. No entries have yet been made in Hoddle Ltd's books of account in respect of these 3 documents.

You are required to state whether these are valid VAT tax invoices and how much input tax (if any) can be claimed in respect of these.

Engineering Supplies Limited

Haddlefield Road, Blaysley, CG6 6AW
Tel/Fax: 01376 44531

Hoddle Limited　　　　　　　　**SALES INVOICE NO:** 2155
22 Formguard Street
Pexley
PY6 3QW

Date: 27 March 20X8

VAT omitted in error from invoice no 2139	
dated 15 March 20X8	£
£2,667.30 @ 20%	533.46
	———
Total due	533.46
	———

Terms: net 30 days

VAT registration: 318 1827 58

Alpha Stationery

Aindsale Centre, Mexton, EV1 4DF
Telephone: 01392 43215

26 March 20X8

1 box transparent folders : red

Total incl VAT @ 20%	14.84
Amount tendered	20.00
Change	5.16

VAT registration: 356 7612 33

JAMIESON & CO

Jamieson House, Baines Road, Gresham, GM7 2PQ
Telephone: 01677 35567   Fax: 01677 57640

PROFORMA SALES INVOICE

VAT registration: 412 7553 67

Hoddle Limited
22 Formguard Street
Pexley
PY6 3QW

For professional services in connection with debt collection

	£
Our fees	350.00
VAT	70.00
Total due	420.00

A VAT invoice will be submitted when the total due is paid in full.

	Valid VAT invoice	Input tax £ p
Engineering Supplies Ltd	YES/NO	
Alpha Stationery	YES/NO	
Jamieson and Co	YES/NO	

Workbook Activity 13

A manufacturing business supplies a mixture of standard rated and reduced rated goods to a VAT registered customer.

Which one of the following statements is true?

A   The business must issue separate VAT invoices for the standard rated and reduced rated goods

B   A single VAT invoice can be issued showing the VAT applicable to standard rated and reduced rated goods as a single amount

C   A single VAT invoice can be issued showing the VAT applicable to standard rated and reduced rated goods as separate amounts

D   A single VAT invoice can be issued showing separate VAT inclusive amounts for standard rated and reduced rated goods without the VAT itself being shown separately

Input and output tax

Introduction

This chapter deals with some of the special rules for recovering input tax and charging output tax.

It also explains what happens when a business makes both taxable and exempt supplies and is therefore partially exempt.

KNOWLEDGE
Recognise different types of inputs and outputs (1.5)
Identify how different types of supply are classified for VAT purposes (1.6)
SKILLS
Calculate accurately relevant inputs and outputs (1.2)

CONTENTS

1 Recovery of input tax
2 Output tax – capital assets
3 Partial exemption

1 Recovery of input tax

1.1 Conditions

Input VAT is usually recoverable by registered traders on goods and services which are supplied to them. In order to recover the input tax the following conditions must be met:

- The goods or services must be supplied for business purposes. Traders cannot recover input VAT on items bought for personal use.

- A VAT invoice is usually needed to support the claim.

- The input VAT must not be 'blocked' (i.e. irrecoverable).

Note that there is no distinction between revenue and capital expenditure for VAT.

Input VAT can be recovered on purchases of capital assets as well as revenue expenditure provided the conditions above are satisfied.

1.2 Irrecoverable (blocked) input VAT

Input VAT on the following goods and services cannot be recovered:

- Most forms of business entertaining.

- Purchase of cars, unless they are 100% used for business purposes (e.g. car owned by a driving school purely used to give driving lessons or a pool car used by employees).

  However, VAT can be recovered on the purchase of commercial vehicles like vans and lorries.

1.3 Business entertaining

In general a business cannot recover input VAT on entertaining. However, there are some cases where VAT on entertaining **can** be recovered.

- Employee entertaining (e.g. staff parties, staff outings and team building events).

  If non employees are included, the business can only recover input VAT on the proportion of the expenses that relate to employees.

- VAT on entertaining overseas customers can be recovered.

Reference material

Information about VAT on vehicles and entertainment expenses is included in the official VAT reference material provided in the real assessment, so you do not need to learn it.

You need to be familiar with the location and content of the material as in the assessment you will need to access the correct part of the reference material from a series of clickable links.

Why not look up the correct part of the Official Reference Material in the Appendix to this textbook now?

Activity 1

You are given the following information about business costs for the quarter to 31.12.X1.

Complete the table to show the amount of input tax that can be reclaimed on each item (to the nearest pence).

All items are standard rated for VAT purposes.

	Item	VAT inclusive cost £ p	Input tax recoverable £ p
1	Car to be used by the managing director 60% for business and 40% privately.	16,600.00	
2	Delivery van	17,500.00	
3	Staff party – staff were each allowed to bring a guest. Half the cost is estimated to be for these guests.	630.00	
4	Entertaining UK customers and suppliers	526.00	
5	Car to be used as a pool car (i.e. available for all employees and kept at the business premises)	11,475.00	

1.4 Motor expenses

Even though businesses cannot usually recover input VAT on the purchase cost of a car, a business can recover input VAT incurred on the running costs of a car such as fuel and repairs. This applies even when there is some private use of the car.

When a business pays fuel costs for an employee or sole trader, and there is some private use of the vehicle, extra output tax will be payable.

This extra output tax is called a **fuel scale charge** and varies with the CO_2 emissions of the car. The fuel scale charge is a **VAT inclusive figure** so the VAT element is calculated as 1/6. However, the scale charge tables supplied by HMRC do this calculation for you.

Note that the scale charges are given in 5 g/km intervals. If a car has an emission figure which is not exactly equal to one of the scale charges on the list, then it has to be rounded down to the next lower figure.

 Example

Forge Ltd provides a company car to Charles and pays for all his private fuel. The CO_2 emission level of the car is 204 g/km.

The scale charge table shows (for a 3 month period):

200 g/km	£500	VAT £83.33
205 g/km	£517	VAT £86.17

The scale figure for 200 g/km is used as 204 g/km is rounded down to 200. The VAT exclusive amount of £416.67 (£500 – £83.33) will be added to the total outputs on the company's VAT return (See Chapter 7) and additional output tax of £83.33 will be payable by the company.

Note that for assessment purposes, you need to be aware of the fuel scale charges and the effect on the total VAT payable / reclaimable, but detailed calculations will not be required.

If a business does not want to pay a fuel scale charge then they can either:

(a)　reclaim only VAT on business fuel (detailed records of business and private mileage need to be kept to prove the business mileage), or

(b)　not claim any VAT on fuel at all even for commercial vehicles. This has the advantage of being simple and is useful if mileage is low.

Reference material

Information about recovering VAT on road fuel is included in the official VAT reference material provided in the real assessment, so you do not need to learn it.

You need to be familiar with the location and content of the material as in the assessment you will need to access the correct part of the reference material from a series of clickable links.

Why not look up the correct part of the Official Reference Material in the Appendix to this textbook now?

2 Output tax – capital assets

2.1 Introduction

Registered traders must charge output tax on all taxable supplies at the appropriate rate. This includes sales of capital assets as well as normal revenue sales.

2.2 Sales of capital assets

Normally when a registered trader sells a capital asset they will charge VAT at the standard rate on the sale price.

However if the asset is a car on which the input tax was blocked (i.e. the trader could not recover the input tax), then no output VAT is charged as it is an exempt sale.

If the input VAT was recoverable on the car, then output VAT is charged on the sale price as normal.

Activity 2

You are given the following information about sales of capital assets in the quarter to 31.12.X1.

Complete the table to show the amount of output tax that must be charged on each item (to the nearest pence).

Item	Input tax recovered	Sale proceeds (excl VAT) £	Output tax £ p
Van	Yes	11,000	2200
Car (1)	Yes	9,500	1900
Car (2)	No	10,550	0
Machinery	Yes	21,000	4200

3 Partial exemption

3.1 Partial exemption

A taxable person who makes both taxable supplies and exempt supplies is referred to as a **partially exempt** trader. For this purpose it does not matter if the taxable supplies are standard or zero rated.

The problem with partial exemption is that taxable supplies entitle the supplier to a credit for input tax in respect of related costs, whereas exempt supplies do not.

It is therefore necessary to apportion input tax between taxable and exempt supplies using a method set out by HMRC.

The most common method used is to divide input tax into three parts:

- Relating wholly to taxable supplies – all recoverable
- Relating wholly to exempt supplies – irrecoverable (but see below)
- Relating to overheads – proportion which relate to taxable supplies can be recovered, leaving the rest irrecoverable (but see below).

If the total irrecoverable input tax is no more than a certain amount, the **de minimis limit**, then it **can** be recovered.

Note that for assessment purposes, you need an awareness of the basics of this topic but calculations of the amount of exempt input tax will not be required.

Reference material

This information is included in the official VAT reference material provided in the real assessment, so you do not need to learn it.

You need to be familiar with the location and content of the material as in the assessment you will need to access the correct part of the reference material from a series of clickable links.

Why not look up the correct part of the Official Reference Material in the Appendix to this textbook now?

---

4 Summary

This chapter has looked at the rules for recovering input tax and examined the items which have a restricted recovery.

Cars with some private use and business entertaining are the examples of 'blocked' input tax that you are required to know for your assessment. There are some exceptions for entertaining.

The treatment of motor expenses is also an important area and you should be aware of the different treatments possible.

Finally the chapter deals with the topic of partially exempt businesses. Such businesses may have to restrict the amount of input tax they can recover

5   Test your knowledge

 Workbook Activity 3

A business supplies goods that are a mixture of standard rated and exempt. Which one of the following statements is true?

A   All of the input VAT can be reclaimed

B   None of the input VAT can be reclaimed

C   All of the input VAT can be reclaimed provided certain de minimis conditions are met ✓

D   Only the input VAT on goods and services purchased for use in making standard rated supplies can ever be reclaimed

Workbook Activity 4

You are given the following information about sales of capital assets in the quarter to 31.12.X1.

Complete the table to show the amount of output tax that must be charged on each item (to the nearest pence).

Item	Input tax recovered	Sale proceeds (excl VAT) £	Output tax £ P
Computer	Yes	2,100	
Car	No	10,000	
Van	Yes	12,500	
Motorcycle	Yes	6,760	

Workbook Activity 5

Scott Ltd provides a car to an employee who uses it for both private and business use. All running expenses of the car are paid for by the company including fuel.

Which one of the following statements is true?

A   There are no VAT implications

B   The company can recover all of the input tax on the running costs and need take no further action

C   The company can recover all of the input tax on the running costs of the car and must add an amount to output tax determined by a scale charge

D   The company cannot recover input tax on running costs of the car but must add an amount to output tax determined by a scale charge

 Workbook Activity 6

You are given the following information about purchases and expenses of a manufacturing business in the quarter to 30.6.X1.

Select Yes or No in the final column to show if the input tax on each item can be reclaimed.

Description	Input VAT £ p	Reclaim input VAT?
Car – for personal use by employee	1,960.00	Yes/No
Overseas customer entertainment	235.50	Yes/No
Staff party	142.70	Yes/No
Office supplies	27.45	Yes/No
Lorry	4,000.00	Yes/No

VAT accounting schemes

5

Introduction

This chapter deals with VAT accounting. There are several special schemes available for small businesses. These schemes have a number of advantages. They can reduce administration (annual accounting and flat rate scheme) or improve cash flow (cash accounting).

You should pay particular attention to which businesses are eligible and the reasons why a business might join one of these schemes.

KNOWLEDGE
Explain the requirements and the frequency of reporting for the following VAT schemes: annual accounting; cash accounting; flat rate scheme; standard scheme (1.7)

SKILLS
Complete accurately and submit a VAT return within the statutory time limits along with any associated payments (1.5)

CONTENTS

1 Standard scheme
2 Annual accounting
3 Cash accounting
4 The flat rate scheme

1 Standard scheme

1.1 Return periods

All registered traders have to complete a VAT return every return period. Information to complete the return is taken from sales and purchase information – usually from daybook totals. Any amounts of VAT due must be paid over to HMRC or a claim made for VAT to be reimbursed.

Return periods are normally 3 months, but traders who regularly receive repayments may elect for monthly return periods.

1.2 Submission of returns

Returns must normally be submitted to **arrive with HMRC** one month after the end of the return period.

Traders who submit their returns online, rather than using a paper return, usually get an extra 7 days to submit.

Since 1.4.2012 all traders (with a few exceptions) must submit their returns online, and pay their VAT electronically.

Completion of VAT returns is dealt with in Chapter 7.

1.3 Payment of VAT

The due date for payment of VAT depends on whether the trader is paying by sending a cheque through the post or paying electronically.

Postal payments can only be made with paper VAT returns and payment is due at the same time as the return, i.e. payments must have cleared HMRC bank account by **one month after the end of the return period.** Paper VAT returns are now very rare.

Electronic payments **must** be made if returns are submitted online and **may** be made when paper returns are submitted. The payment date is normally 7 days later than for a postal payment.

This extra 7 days does not apply:

- if the trader uses the annual accounting scheme.
- if the trader has to make monthly payments (compulsory for large businesses).

Example

Jonas has a quarterly return period to 30 April.

If Jonas submits a paper VAT return it must be with HMRC by 31 May. If he submits electronically he will have until 7 June to submit.

If Jonas submits a paper return he can send a cheque with his return to clear HMRC's bank account by 31 May. Otherwise he must pay electronically by 7 June.

If you pay by direct debit the payment is taken from your account three working days after the 7 day period allowed for electronic payments.

Other electronic payment methods include:

- By debit or credit card over the internet
- Telephone banking payments
- BACS direct credit
- Bank Giro

 Reference material

Information on submission and payment dates is included in the official VAT reference material provided in the real assessment, so you do not need to learn it.

You need to be familiar with the location and content of the material as in the assessment you will need to access the correct part of the reference material from a series of clickable links.

Why not look up the correct part of the Official Reference Material in the Appendix to this textbook now?

1.4 Other schemes

There are a number of special schemes for accounting for VAT. These are designed to help small businesses by reducing administration and may improve cash flow. The schemes which you must know about are:

- annual accounting
- cash accounting
- the flat rate scheme.

There are also special schemes for retailers and businesses that sell second-hand goods. However you do not need to know details of these.

2   Annual accounting

2.1   Purpose of the scheme

Smaller businesses may find it costly or inconvenient to prepare the normal four quarterly VAT returns.

An 'annual' accounting scheme is available whereby a single VAT return is filed for a 12-month period (normally the accounting period of the business). This helps relieve the burden of administration.

2.2   How the scheme works

Only one VAT return is submitted each year, but VAT payments must still be made regularly. The scheme works as follows:

- The annual return must be filed within 2 months of the end of the annual return period..

- Normally, nine payments on account of the VAT liability for the year are made at the end of months 4 to 12 of the year. Each payment represents 10% of the VAT liability for the previous year..

- A new business will base its payments on an estimate of the VAT liability for the year.

- Businesses may apply to HMRC to agree quarterly payments on account instead of the normal nine monthly payments. In this case, the payments will be 25% of the VAT liability for the previous year and will be made by the ends of months 4, 7 and 10.

- A balancing payment or repayment is made when the return is filed.

- All payments must be made electronically with no 7 days extension.

- Additional payments can be made by the business when desired.

2.3   Conditions for the annual accounting scheme

The scheme is aimed at smaller businesses.

- Businesses can join the scheme provided their taxable turnover (excluding VAT and the sale of capital assets) expected in the next 12 months is no more than £1,350,000.

- The business must be up-to-date with its VAT returns. However a business does not need a history of VAT returns to join. It can join the scheme from the day it registers.

- Businesses must leave the scheme if their estimated taxable turnover (excluding VAT) for the next 12 months is more than £1,600,000.

2.4 Who might use the scheme?

The scheme is useful to businesses that want to:

- reduce administration because only one VAT return is needed instead of four and businesses get 2 months to prepare the return instead of the usual one.

- fix their VAT payments in advance, at least for their nine monthly or three quarterly payments. This is useful for budgeting cash flow.

It is not useful if:

- the business receives repayments as only one repayment per year will be received.

- the business turnover decreases, as then the interim payments might be higher than under the standard scheme and the business will have to wait until they submit the VAT return to get any repayment due.

Activity 1

Jump Ltd applies to use the annual accounting scheme from 1 January 20X1. The company's net VAT liability for the year ended 31 December 20X0 was £3,600.00.

The actual net VAT liability for the year ended 31 December 20X1 is £3,820.00.

1 When must Jump Ltd's VAT return be filed?

    A   31 January 20X2

    B   28 February 20X2

    C   31 March 20X2

2 Which ONE of the following statements about Jump Ltd's payment of VAT during the year ended 31 December 20X1 is true?

    Assume Jump Ltd has not chosen quarterly payments.

    A   Jump Ltd must make nine monthly payments of £360.00

    B   Jump Ltd must make nine monthly payments of £382.00

    C   Jump Ltd must make twelve monthly payments of £300.00

    D   Jump Ltd must make twelve monthly payments of £318.33

3 What is the balancing payment/repayment due from/to Jump Ltd when their VAT return for the year ended 31 December 20X1 is filed?

> **Reference material**
>
> Information about annual accounting is included in the official VAT reference material provided in the real assessment, so you do not need to learn it.
>
> You need to be familiar with the location and content of the material as in the assessment you will need to access the correct part of the reference material from a series of clickable links.
>
> Why not look up the correct part of the Official Reference Material in the Appendix to this textbook now?

3 Cash accounting

3.1 How the scheme works

Normally VAT is accounted for on the basis of invoices issued and received in a return period. Accordingly:

- Output VAT is paid to HMRC by reference to the period in which the tax point occurs (usually the delivery or invoice date), regardless of whether payment has been received from the customer.

- Input VAT is reclaimed from HMRC by reference to the invoices received in the return period, even if payment has not been made to the supplier.

However, under the cash accounting scheme a business accounts for VAT on the basis of when payment is actually received from customers or made to suppliers. The tax point becomes the date of receipt or payment.

If registered under the scheme invoices will still be sent to customers and received from suppliers in the normal way, but the key record that must be kept is a cash book. This should summarise all the payments made and received and have a **separate column for VAT.**

3.2 Conditions

As with annual accounting, the scheme is aimed at smaller businesses. The conditions are:

- The trader's VAT returns must be up-to-date and they must have no convictions for VAT offences or penalties for dishonest conduct.

- Estimated taxable turnover, excluding VAT and sales of capital assets, must not exceed £1,350,000 for the next year.

- Once in the scheme, a trader must leave once their annual taxable turnover, excluding VAT, exceeds £1,600,000.

- When they leave the scheme they must account for all outstanding VAT (i.e. on debtors less creditors), as they will be moving to a system where VAT is accounted for on invoices not on a cash basis.

3.3 Advantages and disadvantages

Advantages	Disadvantages
• Businesses selling on credit do not have to pay output VAT to HMRC until they receive it from customers.	• Input tax cannot be claimed until the invoice is paid. This delays recovery of input VAT.
• This gives automatic bad debt relief because if the customer does not pay, then the VAT on their invoice is not paid over to HMRC. Cash flow is improved.	• Not suitable for businesses with a lot of cash sales or zero-rated supplies. Using cash accounting in these situations just causes a delay in the recovery of input VAT.
• Cash accounting can be used with annual accounting.	• If a business uses cash accounting as soon as it registers, it will be unable to reclaim VAT on stock and assets until the invoices for these items are paid.

Activity 2

Would each of the following businesses benefit from joining the cash accounting scheme? Select Yes or No for each business.

1   JB Ltd which operates a retail shop selling directly to the public. All sales are for cash and all purchases are made on credit. JB Ltd's supplies are all standard rated.   YES/NO

2   Amber and Co, which manufactures and sells computer printers to other businesses. This is a standard rated business and all sales and purchases are made on credit.   YES/NO

3   John Smith, a sole trader who manufactures children's shoes and sells them to retailers. This is a zero-rated activity and all sales and purchases are made on credit.   YES/NO

> **Reference material**
>
> Information about cash accounting is included in the official VAT reference material provided in the real assessment, so you do not need to learn it.
>
> You need to be familiar with the location and content of the material as in the assessment you will need to access the correct part of the reference material from a series of clickable links.
>
> Why not look up the correct part of the Official Reference Material in the Appendix to this textbook now?

4 The flat rate scheme

4.1 Purpose of the scheme

The optional flat rate scheme is aimed at simplifying the way in which very small businesses calculate their VAT liability.

4.2 How the scheme works

Under the flat rate scheme, a business **calculates its VAT liability** by simply applying a flat rate percentage to total turnover. This removes the need to calculate and record output and input VAT. In some cases it can save the business money.

- The flat rate percentage is applied to the gross (VAT inclusive) **total turnover** figure. This includes standard rated, zero rated and exempt supplies. No input VAT is recovered.

- The percentage varies according to the type of trade in which the business is involved. In their first year in the scheme a business gets a 1% discount on their normal percentage. If you need to know a percentage in the assessment it will be given to you.

- A **VAT invoice must still be issued** to customers and VAT charged at the appropriate rate.

- A VAT account must still be maintained.

- The flat rate scheme is **only** used to calculate the VAT due to HMRC.

- The flat rate scheme can be used together with the annual accounting scheme.

- It is not possible to join both the flat rate scheme and the cash accounting scheme, however it is possible to request that the flat rate scheme calculations are performed on a cash paid/ receipts basis.

4.3   Conditions for the scheme

In order to join the scheme, the **taxable** turnover of the business, (excluding VAT), for the next 12 months, must not be expected to exceed £150,000.

Once in the scheme, a business can stay in until their **tax inclusive** turnover (**including taxable and exempt income**) for the previous 12 months exceeds £230,000.

 Example

Simon runs a business selling computer supplies. He has joined the flat rate scheme.

If the flat rate percentage for this type of business is 12%, how much VAT should Simon pay over for the quarter ended 30 June 20X0 when his turnover (including VAT) is £39,000?

Solution

£4,680.00 (£39,000 × 12%)

4.4   Advantages and disadvantages of the flat rate scheme

The advantages of the scheme include the following:

- A business does not have to record the VAT charged on each individual sale and purchase.

- Easier administration as the business does not have to decide which amounts of input VAT can be reclaimed and which cannot.

- The business gets a discount of 1% in the first year.

- The business may pay less VAT than using the standard method.

- The business has certainty as the percentage of turnover that has to be paid over as VAT is known in advance.

- There is less chance of making a mistake in calculating VAT.

The percentage used in flat rate accounting is fixed for particular trade sectors and takes into account the mix of standard rated, zero rated and exempt sales made by the average business in that sector.

The scheme may not be suitable for businesses which do not have the same mix as an average business.

In particular it would not be suitable for:

- businesses that regularly receive repayments under standard VAT accounting

- businesses that buy a higher proportion of standard rated items than others in their trade sector as they would not be able to reclaim the input VAT on these purchases

- businesses that make a higher proportion of zero rated or exempt sales than others in their trade.

 Activity 3

In the year ended 31 December 20X0, Apple Ltd has annual sales to the general public of £100,000, all of which are standard rated.

The company incurs standard rated expenses of £4,500 per annum

These figures include VAT at 20%.

1   What is Apple Ltd's VAT liability using the standard method?

     A   £19,100.00

     B   £15,916.66

     C   £20,000.00

     D   £16,666.66

2   What is Apple Ltd's VAT liability using the flat rate method assuming a percentage of 9%?

     A   £20,000.00

     B   £16,666.66

     C   £9,000.00

     D   £8,595.00

Reference material

Information about the flat rate scheme is included in the official VAT reference material provided in the real assessment, so you do not need to learn it.

You need to be familiar with the location and content of the material as in the assessment you will need to access the correct part of the reference material from a series of clickable links.

Why not look up the correct part of the Official Reference Material in the Appendix to this textbook now?

5 Summary

Clearly it is important for a business to know when they have to complete VAT returns and pay over VAT. The normal pattern is to complete returns and pay over VAT quarterly or monthly. This is the case unless the business has chosen annual accounting which is one of the special schemes aimed at smaller businesses.

Annual accounting gives the advantages of only one annual VAT return and fixed regular VAT payments. The turnover limits for the scheme are the same as for cash accounting.

Cash accounting changes the normal tax point rules and allows the business to pay over VAT when they actually receive the cash from their customers rather than the delivery or invoice date. This gives automatic bad debt relief but has the disadvantage that input VAT can only be claimed when suppliers are paid.

The flat rate scheme is aimed at simplifying VAT accounting for the very small business. The amount of VAT payable is determined by simply applying a fixed percentage to the VAT inclusive turnover of the business. However it is important to remember that the business still has to comply with the rules about issuing tax invoices.

6 Test your knowledge

Workbook Activity 4

Indicate whether the following statements about the flat rate scheme are true or false.

Tick one box on each line.

		True	False
1	VAT invoices are not issued to customers.		✓
2	A VAT account need not be kept.		✓
3	Traders using the flat rate scheme can also join the annual accounting scheme.	✓	
4	Traders can join the flat rate scheme if their taxable turnover for the last 12 months is below £230,000.		✓
5	The flat rate scheme percentage varies according to the trade sector of the business.	✓	

Workbook Activity 5

A VAT registered business has a year end of 30 June 20X2 and uses the annual accounting scheme.

1 Which one of the following statements is true?

A The whole VAT liability for the year is payable on 30 June 20X2

B The whole VAT liability for the year is payable on 31 August 20X2

C The VAT liability is payable in nine monthly instalments starting on 31 October 20X1 with a balancing payment on 31 July 20X2

D The VAT liability is payable in nine monthly instalments starting on 31 October 20X1 with a balancing payment on 31 August 20X2

2 The annual VAT return is due to be submitted by which date?

A 31 July 20X2

B 31 August 20X2

 Workbook Activity 6

Oak Ltd has prepared its VAT return for the quarter ended 30 September.

1 When is Oak Ltd's return due assuming it does not submit its returns electronically?

A 14 October

B 30 October

C 31 October

D 7 November

2 What would be the due date for submission of the return if Oak Ltd submitted it electronically?

A 14 October

B 31 October

C 6 November

D 7 November

Workbook Activity 7

Which one of the following is not an advantage of the flat rate scheme?

A   The business gets a discount of 1% on the flat rate percentage in the first year

B   VAT returns do not need to be completed

C   The business does not have to record the VAT charged on individual sales and purchases

D   The business has easier administration as it does not have to decide which input VAT can be reclaimed and which cannot

 Workbook Activity 8

Indicate whether the following statements about the cash accounting scheme are true or false.

Tick one box on each line.

		True	False
1	VAT invoices are not issued to customers		✓
2	The scheme gives automatic bad debt relief	✓	
3	Cash accounting is useful for businesses with a high proportion of cash sales	✓	⌀
4	If a business adopts cash accounting then their customers cannot reclaim input VAT until they pay their invoices	✓	⌀
5	A business cannot join the cash accounting scheme if their VAT returns are not up to date	⌀	✓

Workbook Activity 9

In the year ended 31 December 20X1, Pear Ltd has annual sales of £80,000, all of which are standard rated and to the general public.

The company incurs standard rated expenses of £6,100 per annum.

These figures are VAT exclusive.

1   Select which of the following gives Pear Ltd's liability using the standard method.

    A   £12,316.66

    B   £16,000.00

    C   £14,780.00

    D   £14,983.34

2   Select which of the following gives Pear Ltd's VAT liability using the flat rate method assuming a percentage of 8%.

    A   £6,400.00

    B   £7,680.00

13333

1220

Workbook Activity 10

1   Which one of the following statements is true?

    A   Traders using the standard accounting scheme normally submit their VAT returns every quarter

    B   Electronic VAT returns must be submitted 7 days after the end of the return period

    C   A trader is always permitted to pay VAT by sending a cheque through the post

2   What is the annual turnover limit for eligibility to join the annual accounting scheme?

    A   £1,350,000

    B   £1,600,000

3   John's VAT liability for the previous year was £7,200.00. He estimates it will be £7,800.00 this year. He joins the annual accounting scheme and elects to pay by quarterly instalments. What is the size of each instalment?

    A   £1,800.00

    B   £1,950.00

4   Which one of the following statements about cash accounting is false?

    A   Cash accounting is a disadvantage for a business selling zero rated supplies

    B   VAT invoices need not be sent out

    C   The key record for determining VAT due is the cash book

5   Zak is a registered trader using the flat rate scheme with a percentage of 12%. His sales for the quarter are all standard rated and are £75,000 inclusive of VAT at 20%.

    What VAT should he pay over for the quarter?

    A   £9,000.00

    B   £7,500.00

VAT errors and penalties

Introduction

This chapter is a short one explaining what happens if a business does not abide by all the VAT regulations.

Correction of errors is also covered. This is an important topic and will often be tested in the assessment task dealing with the actual completion of a VAT return.

KNOWLEDGE

Recognise the implications and penalties for the organisation resulting from failure to abide by VAT regulations including the late submission of VAT returns (1.8)

SKILLS

Make adjustments and declarations for any errors or omissions identified in previous VAT periods (1.4)

CONTENTS

1 Tax avoidance and evasion
2 Penalties
3 Default surcharge

1 Tax avoidance and evasion

1.1 Tax avoidance

Tax avoidance means arranging your tax affairs, using legal methods so that you pay less tax. Individuals and businesses can reduce their tax bills by claiming all the reliefs and allowances to which they are entitled. Sometimes a transaction can be timed to give maximum tax advantage.

Tax avoidance is legal.

1.2 Tax evasion

Tax evasion, however, is a criminal offence.

Tax evasion means using illegal methods to reduce tax due. Typically this might be through concealing a source of income, deliberately understating income or over-claiming expenses and reliefs. VAT could be evaded by under-declaring or concealing outputs and output tax or by overstating inputs and hence over-claiming input tax.

VAT evasion is a criminal offence, but in many cases HMRC prefer to claim penalties and interest rather than pursue cases through the courts.

2 Penalties

2.1 Introduction

VAT has many regulations with which a business must comply. As mentioned in Chapter 1, HMRC have powers to check whether a business is keeping to the rules.

- HMRC make occasional control visits to check that returns are correct.

- HMRC have the power to enter business premises and inspect records and documents.

If a business fails to comply with VAT regulations they will usually receive a penalty (fine). The amount of the penalty varies according to the offence, but in recent years HMRC has been working to produce a standard penalty system.

For your assessment, you need to know the main principles of the enforcement regime but not the fine detail.

2.2 Summary of main penalties

Offence	Penalty
Failure to register	Standard penalty plus all VAT due from date registration should have taken place
Incorrect return (where error is careless or deliberate)	Standard penalty plus error must be corrected
Late returns and/or late payment	Default surcharge

2.3 Failure to register

Registration rules were dealt with in Chapter 2.

If a business fails to register when it should, then HMRC can issue an assessment asking them to pay over all the VAT due since the date it should have registered, plus a penalty can be levied.

The penalty is determined by the standard penalty regime which applies across all taxes and is a percentage of the VAT outstanding. The percentage to use varies from 0% for genuine mistakes up to 100% for deliberate and concealed actions. The penalty can be reduced if the trader cooperates with HMRC.

2.4 Incorrect return

If a trader makes an error in a VAT return which leads to net VAT payable being understated this must be corrected (see below). A net VAT error is calculated as the difference between VAT due to HMRC less any VAT claimable by the trader.

Note that the amount of any errors or omissions will be given in the assessment.

A penalty may be charged if the error is careless or deliberate.

If a trader discovers a non-careless error, such as a simple mistake, then they must take steps to correct it. If they do not then HMRC will treat it as a careless error and a penalty may be charged.

If a trader does not submit a return at all then HMRC can issue an assessment which estimates the amount of VAT due. If this estimate is too low and a trader does not tell HMRC within 30 days that it is too low, then a penalty can be charged.

Example

Bishop is a registered trader who prepares VAT returns quarterly. He discovers that in his previous quarter he entered VAT output tax on his return as £56,792.00 when it should have been £65,972.00. He also entered input tax as £45,510.00 when it should have been £45,150.00.

He also discovers that he has not reclaimed the VAT of £3,450.00 on the purchase of a new milling machine.

What is the net VAT error?

Solution

	£
Output tax understated (£65,972.00 – £56,792.00)	9,180.00
Input tax overstated (£45,510.00 – £45,150.00)	360.00
Input tax understated – not claimed on machine	(3,450.00)
	————
Net VAT error (extra VAT due)	6,090.00
	————

A penalty under the standard penalty regime may be charged. This will be a percentage of the net VAT understated, and as for late registration, it varies from 0% to 100% of the error.

In addition, interest may be charged.

 Reference material

Some information on penalties is included in the official VAT reference material provided in the real assessment, so you do not need to learn it.

You need to be familiar with the location and content of the material as in the assessment you will need to access the correct part of the reference material from a series of clickable links.

Why not look up the correct part of the Official Reference Material in the Appendix to this textbook now?

2.5 Correcting errors – voluntary disclosure

If a trader discovers that they have made an error in an earlier VAT return then they must try to correct it as soon as possible. There are two methods of correction depending on the size of error.

- Include on next VAT return (only if non deliberate)
- Include on VAT form 652 (or by letter if no form available).

Include on next VAT return	Submit on form 652
Errors can be corrected on the next VAT return if they are: • No more than £10,000; or • Between £10,000 and £50,000 but no more than 1% of turnover for the current return period (specifically the figure included in Box 6 of the VAT return – see Chapter 7)	Errors must be separately disclosed if they: • Exceed £50,000; or • Exceed £10,000 and are more than 1% of the turnover for the current return period (figure in Box 6 of the return) • Any deliberate errors

 Reference material

Error limit information is included in the official VAT reference material provided in the real assessment, so you do not need to learn it.

You need to be familiar with the location and content of the material as in the assessment you will need to access the correct part of the reference material from a series of clickable links.

Why not look up the correct part of the Official Reference Material in the Appendix to this textbook now?

 Activity 1

You are given the following information about the net errors and turnover of four businesses.

For each of them, indicate whether they can correct the error on the next VAT return or whether separate disclosure is required.

Tick ONE box on EACH line.

Assume none of the errors are deliberate.

Net error £ p	Turnover £	Include in VAT return	Separate disclosure
4,500.00	100,000	✓	
12,000.00	250,000		✓
30,000.00	3,500,000	✓	
60,000.00	10,000,000		✓

2.6 Errors found by HMRC

An error may be discovered by HMRC, for example during a VAT control visit. In this case HMRC may issue a discovery assessment (i.e. a demand) to collect any VAT due.

Normally HMRC have up to 4 years after the end of the return period in which the error occurred to issue an assessment. This is extended to 20 years for deliberate behaviour (such as fraud).

HMRC can also issue a penalty under the standard penalty regime and charge interest on the unpaid VAT. Any penalty is likely to be higher than if the trader found the error themselves and voluntarily disclosed it.

2.7 Summary of errors and omissions

Error/omissions	Action
Failing to register	HMRC can issue assessment to collect tax due and charge a penalty
Failure to submit a return	HMRC can issue an assessment to collect tax due
Failure to tell HMRC that an assessment is too low within 30 days	Penalty can be charged
Making a non-careless error	Trader must take steps to correct otherwise error may be regarded as careless
Making a careless or deliberate error	Trader must correct the error. HMRC can charge a penalty.
Correcting errors	Inclusion on form 652 or by letter. If below limit can include on next return.

Error omissions	Action
Errors found by HMRC	HMRC can raise an assessment within 4 years of the end of the VAT period (careless errors) or 20 years (deliberate errors like fraud). A penalty can be charged.
Submitting VAT return late or paying late	Default surcharge regime applies

Reference material

Much of this information is included in the official VAT reference material provided in the real assessment, so you do not need to learn it.

You need to be familiar with the location and content of the material as in the assessment you will need to access the correct part of the reference material from a series of clickable links.

Why not look up the correct part of the Official Reference Material in the Appendix to this textbook now?

3 Default surcharge

3.1 Surcharge liability notice

If a trader commits a **default** by submitting their VAT return late or paying their VAT late, HMRC will serve a **surcharge liability notice.**

This identifies a surcharge period which runs until 12 months after the end of the period for which the trader is in default.

Example

Jolene submits her paper return for the quarter ended 30 June 20X6 on 15 August 20X6 but pays her VAT electronically on 3 August 20X6.

As this is a late return, a surcharge liability notice will be issued by HMRC which will cover the period up to 30 June 20X7.

3.2 Effect of surcharge liability notice

The surcharge liability notice acts as a warning to the trader. If they commit a further default within the surcharge period then:

(i) the surcharge period is extended so it now ends 12 months after the end of the new default period, and

(ii) if the default is a late VAT payment (rather than just a late VAT return), then the trader is charged a **surcharge** penalty which is a fixed percentage of the VAT overdue.

The process is repeated if the trader commits further defaults within the surcharge period, with increasing levels of penalty charged.

Hence the trader needs to stay free of defaults for twelve months to come out of the default surcharge system.

For assessment purposes you are not expected to know how the amount of the surcharge is calculated or what happens if a further default arises in the surcharge period.

Reference material

Some of this information is included in the official VAT reference material provided in the real assessment, so you do not need to learn it.

You need to be familiar with the location and content of the material as in the assessment you will need to access the correct part of the reference material from a series of clickable links.

Why not look up the correct part of the Official Reference Material in the Appendix to this textbook now?

3.3 Reasonable excuse

A surcharge liability notice will not be issued if the trader has a **reasonable excuse** for submitting their return or paying their VAT late.

Examples of reasonable excuse include:

- Computer breakdown just before or during the preparation of the return or loss of records due to fire or flood.

- Illness of an employee who prepares the return where no one else can do the work.

- Sudden cash crisis such as loss of cash due to theft or major customer becoming insolvent.

4 Summary

It is important to know the difference between tax avoidance and evasion as the former is legal and the latter is not.

VAT is a self assessed tax – that is traders calculate their own VAT liability. HMRC have powers to visit businesses and check that they are complying with the rules. If not, penalties can be charged.

For your assessment you need to know the main principles of the enforcement regime, but not the fine detail.

The three main penalties examinable are: late registration, incorrect returns and late submission of VAT returns and payments.

Late registration and errors in returns are dealt with under the common penalty regime. The penalty is not a fixed monetary amount but is determined as a percentage of VAT outstanding. The percentage varies according to the trader's actions and level of cooperation.

The default surcharge applies to late returns and payments. The examiner has stated that you need to know what triggers a surcharge liability notice but you will not be expected to know how the amount of the surcharge is calculated.

Correction of errors is an important area. You will normally be asked to deal with the correction of errors in the assessment task involving completion of the VAT return.

5 Test your knowledge

Workbook Activity 2

1   Tax avoidance is illegal and tax evasion is legal. TRUE or FALSE?

2   Which one of the following is a consequence of submitting an incorrect VAT return?

   A   A penalty may be charged and the error must be corrected on the next VAT return

   B   A penalty may be charged and the error must be corrected by submitting it on form 652

   C   A penalty will be charged and the way in which the error is corrected depends on its size

   D   A penalty may be charged and the way in which the error is corrected depends on its size

3   Tariq finds that he made a non deliberate net error on an earlier VAT return of £12,400.00. If his turnover for the current quarter is £750,000 how should he correct the error?

   A   By inclusion on his next VAT return

   B   By separate notification on form 652 or by letter

4   Fill in the blanks in the following statements.

   A surcharge liability notice runs for 12 months after the end of the return period for which the trader is in default.

   Once the surcharge period has started a VAT default occurs when VAT is paid late

   A surcharge liability notice will not be issued if a trader has a resonable excuse.

Workbook Activity 3

You are given the following information about the non deliberate net errors and turnover of four businesses. For each of them, indicate whether they can correct the error on the next VAT return or whether separate disclosure is required. Tick ONE box on EACH line.

Net error £	Turnover £	Include in VAT return	Separate disclosure
4,500	40,000	✓	
12,500	300,000		✓
40,000	4,500,000	✓	
55,000	6,000,000		✓

Workbook Activity 4

Indicate whether the following statements about VAT errors and penalties are true or false. Tick one box on each line

		True	False
1	If a trader fails to register at the correct time they will have to pay over all the VAT they should have charged to customers since the date they should have been registered.	✓	
2	If a trader makes an error in a VAT return they will always be charged a penalty.		✓
3	A default only occurs if a trader both pays VAT late and submits a VAT return late.		✓
4	Surcharge liability notices cover a period of 12 months.	✓	

7

VAT returns

Introduction

In the last two chapter of this study text we are going to conclude our VAT studies by looking at how to complete a VAT return correctly and on time. Businesses must complete a VAT return (a VAT 100 form) at the end of each quarter. The purpose of a VAT return is to summarise the transactions of a business for a period. In an assessment you will be required to complete an organisation's VAT return so that it is ready for authorisation and despatch.

KNOWLEDGE

Recognise different types of inputs and outputs (1.5)

Identify how different types of supply are classified for VAT purposes (1.6)

SKILLS

Correctly identify and extract relevant data for a specific period from the accounting system (1.1)

Calculate accurately relevant inputs and outputs (1.2)

Calculate accurately the VAT due to, or from, the relevant tax authority (1.3)

Make adjustments and declarations for any errors or omissions identified in previous VAT periods (1.4)

Complete accurately and submit a VAT return within the statutory time limits along with any associated payments (1.5)

Inform managers of the impact that the VAT payment may have on the company cash flow and financial forecasts (2.1)

CONTENTS

1 The VAT return
2 Completing the VAT return
3 Communicating VAT information

1 The VAT return

1.1 Introduction

The tax period for VAT is **three months**, or one month for taxpayers who choose to make monthly returns (normally taxpayers who receive regular refunds).

The taxpayer must complete a **VAT return at the end of each quarter**. The return summarises all the transactions for the period.

1.2 Timing of the VAT return

The taxpayer must submit the return within one month of the end of the tax period (paper) or 1 month and 7 days (electronic). The taxable person must ensure that the amount due (i.e. output tax collected less input tax deducted) clears HMRC bank account at the same time unless a direct debit payment arrangement exists.

For more detail on VAT returns and payments refer back to Chapter **5**.

If VAT is due from HMRC the VAT return must still be completed and submitted to the same time limits as normal in order to be able to reclaim the amount due.

1.3 What a VAT return looks like

Virtually all businesses have to file their returns online rather than on paper.

In the assessment you will have to complete a VAT return which is likely to look as shown in section 1.4.

1.4 VAT return – online style

		£
VAT due in this period on **sales** and other outputs	**Box 1**	3680
VAT due in this period on **acquisitions** from other **EC Member States**	**Box 2**	
Total VAT due (**the sum of boxes 1 and 2**)	**Box 3**	
VAT reclaimed in the period on **purchases** and other inputs, including acquisitions from the EC	**Box 4**	
Net VAT to be paid to HM Revenue & Customs or reclaimed by you (**Difference between boxes 3 and 4**)	**Box 5**	
Total value of **sales** and all other outputs excluding any VAT. **Include your box 8 figure**	**Box 6**	
Total value of purchases and all other inputs excluding any VAT. **Include your box 9 figure**	**Box 7**	
Total value of all **supplies** of goods and related costs, excluding any VAT, to other **EC Member States**	**Box 8**	
Total value of all **acquisitions** of goods and related costs, excluding any VAT, from other **EC Member States**	**Box 9**	

As you will see there are nine boxes to complete with the relevant figures.

Boxes 2, 8 and 9 are to do with supplies of goods and services to other European Union (EU) Member States and acquisitions from EU Member States. These will be considered in Chapter 8.

Note that the EU was formerly known as the EC (European Community) and the VAT returns still use the previous name.

2 Completing the VAT return

2.1 The VAT account

The main source of information for the VAT return is the VAT account which must be maintained to show the amount that is due to or from HMRC at the end of each quarter.

It is important to realise that the balance on the VAT account should agree to the balance of VAT payable/reclaimable on the VAT return.

In the assessment you will not be required to complete a VAT account but you may be asked to select reasons why there is a difference between the balance on the VAT account and on the balance per the VAT return.

2.2 How the VAT account should look

Given below is a pro-forma of a VAT account as suggested by the VAT Guide.

1 April 20X5 to 30 June 20X5			
VAT deductible – input tax		**VAT payable – output tax**	
	£ p		£ p
VAT on purchases		VAT on sales	
April	X	April	X
May	X	May	X
June	X	June	X
VAT on imports	X		
VAT on acquisition from EC	X	VAT on acquisition from EC	X
Adjustments of previous errors			
(if within the error limit – Chapter 6)			
Net under claim	X	Net over claim	X
Bad debt relief (section 2.6)	X		
Less: Credit notes received	(X)	Less: Credit notes issued	(X)
Total tax deductible	X	Total tax payable	X
		Less: Total tax deductible	(X)
		Payable to HMRC	X

The VAT account is part of the double entry system. However, the VAT on credit notes received in this example is deducted from input tax and the VAT on credit notes issued is deducted from output tax instead of being credited and debited respectively. This is because this is how credit notes are dealt with in the VAT return. However, businesses do not have to prepare their VAT account in exactly this way.

 Reference material

Information about the contents of a VAT account is included in the official VAT reference material provided in the real assessment, so you do not need to learn it.

You need to be familiar with the location and content of the material as in the assessment you will need to access the correct part of the reference material from a series of clickable links.

Why not look up the correct part of the Official Reference Material in the Appendix to this textbook now?

2.3 Information required for the VAT return

Boxes 1 to 4 of the VAT return can be fairly easily completed from the information in the VAT account. However, Boxes 6 and 7 require figures for total sales and purchases excluding VAT.

This information will need to be extracted from the totals of the accounting records such as sales day book and purchases day book totals. It is also possible that information relating to VAT could be shown in a journal.

Boxes 8 and 9 require figures, excluding VAT, for the value of supplies to other EC Member States and acquisitions from other EC Member States (dealt with in Chapter 8).

Therefore the accounting records should be designed in such a way that these figures can also be easily identified.

Activity 1

Panther

You are preparing the VAT return for Panther Alarms Ltd and you must first identify the sources of information for the VAT account.

Here is a list of possible sources of accounting information.

1   Sales day book ✓

2   Sales returns day book ✓

3   Bad and doubtful debts account ✓

4   Purchase returns day book ✓

5   Drawings account

6   Purchases day book ✓

7   Cash book

8   Assets account

9   Petty cash book

Select from the list the best sources of information for the following figures by entering a number against each.

If you think the information will be in more than one place then give the number for both.

A   sales   *1*

B   cash sales   *7*

C   credit notes issued   *2*

D   purchases   *6*

E   cash purchases   *7 8 9*

F   credit notes received *6*

G   capital goods sold   *8 8 1*

H   capital goods purchased *8 8 6*

I   bad debt relief   *3*

Example

Given below is a VAT account for Thompson Brothers for the second VAT quarter of 20X5.

Thompson Brothers Ltd   **1 April 20X5 to 30 June 20X5**

VAT deductible – input tax		VAT payable – output tax	
VAT on purchases	£	*VAT on sales*	£
April	700.00	April	1,350.00
May	350.00	May	1,750.00
June	350.00	June	700.00
	1,400.00		3,800.00

Other adjustments

Less: Credit notes received	(20.00)	Less: Credit notes issued	(120.00)
Total tax deductible	1,380.00	Total tax payable	3,680.00
		Less: Total tax deductible	(1,380.00)
		Payable to HMRC	2,300.00

You are also given the summarised totals from the day books for the three-month period:

Sales Day Book

	Net £	VAT £	Total £
Standard rated	19,000.00	3,800.00	22,800.00
Zero rated	800.00	–	800.00

Sales Returns Day Book

	Net £	VAT £	Total £
Standard rated	600.00	120.00	720.00
Zero rated	40.00	–	40.00

Purchases Day Book

	Net £	VAT £	Total £
Standard rated	7,000.00	1,400.00	8,400.00
Zero rated	2,000.00	–	2,000.00

Purchases Returns Day Book

	Net £	VAT £	Total £
Standard rated	100.00	20.00	120.00
Zero rated	–	–	–

We are now in a position to complete the VAT return.

Solution

Step 1

Fill in Box 1 with the VAT on sales less the VAT on credit notes issued.

This can be taken either from the VAT account or from the day book summaries:
(£3,800 – £120) = £3,680.00.

Note that the figures in Boxes 1 – 5 should include pence so put '00' if there are no pence in the total.

Step 2

Fill in Box 2 with the VAT payable on acquisitions from other EC Member states – none here

Step 3

Complete Box 3 with the total of Boxes 1 and 2:
(£3,680.00 + £Nil) = £3,680.00.

Step 4

Fill in Box 4 with the total of VAT on all purchases less the total VAT on any credit notes received. These figures can either be taken from the VAT account or from the day book totals:
(£1,400.00 – £20.00) = £1,380.00.

Step 5

Complete Box 5 by deducting the figure in Box 4 from the total in Box 3:
(£3,680.00 – £1,380.00) = £2,300.00.
This is the amount due to HMRC and should equal the balance on the VAT account.

KAPLAN PUBLISHING

If the Box 4 figure is larger than the Box 3 total then there is more input tax reclaimable than output tax to pay – this means that this is the amount being reclaimed from HMRC.

Step 6

Fill in Box 6 with the VAT exclusive figure of all sales less credit notes issued – this information will come from the day books:
(£19,000 + £800 – £600 – £40) = £19,160

Note that this figure includes zero-rated supplies and any exempt supplies that are made.

Note that the figures in Boxes 6 – 9 should be whole pounds only. In the assessment it does not matter if the numbers are rounded up or down.

Step 7

Fill in Box 7 with the VAT exclusive total of all purchases less credit notes received – again this will be taken from the day books:
(£7,000 + £2,000 – £100) = £8,900

Step 8

Boxes 8 and 9 are for transactions with EC member states. These are dealt with in Chapter 8.

Note that if there is no entry for any box then 0 should be written in the box.

Step 9

If VAT is due to HMRC then payment must be made in accordance with the usual time limits. For assessment purposes you may be asked to state the payment date, or complete an email advising when this amount will be paid.

		£
VAT due in this period on **sales** and other outputs	Box 1	3,630.00
VAT due in this period on **acquisitions** from other **EC Member States**	Box 2	0.00
Total VAT due (**the sum of boxes 1 and 2**)	Box 3	3,630.00
VAT reclaimed in the period on **purchases** and other inputs, including acquisitions from the EC	Box 4	1,380.00
Net VAT to be paid to HM Revenue & Customs or reclaimed by you (**Difference between boxes 3 and 4**)	Box 5	2,300.00
Total value of **sales** and all other outputs excluding any VAT. **Include your box 8 figure**	Box 6	19,160
Total value of purchases and all other inputs excluding any VAT. **Include your box 9 figure**	Box 7	6,900
Total value of all **supplies** of goods and related costs, excluding any VAT, to other **EC Member States**	Box 8	0
Total value of all **acquisitions** of goods and related costs, excluding any VAT, from other **EC Member States**	Box 9	0

If the business makes sales or purchases for cash then the relevant net and VAT figures from the cash receipts and payments books should also be included on the VAT return.

Activity 2

Given below is the summary of relevant ledger accounts for a business for the three months ended 31 March 20X1.

SALES AND SALES RETURNS ACCOUNT					
Date 20X1	Reference	Debit £	Date 20X1	Reference	Credit £
1/1 to 31/03	SRDB Sales returns Std rated	1,625.77	1/1 to 31/03	SDB Std rated sales	15,485.60
1/1 to 31/03	SRDB Sales returns Zero rated	106.59	1/1 to 31/03	SDB Zero rated sales	1,497.56
31/03	Bal c/d	15,250.80			
	Total	16,983.16		Total	16,983.16

PURCHASES AND PURCHASE RETURNS ACCOUNT					
Date 20X1	Reference	Debit £	Date 20X1	Reference	Credit £
1/1 to 31/03	PDB Std rated purchases	8,127.45	1/1 to 31/03	PRDB Purchase returns Std rated	935.47
1/1 to 31/03	PDB Zero rated purchases	980.57	1/1 to 31/03	PRDB Purchase returns zero rated	80.40
			31/03	Bal c/d	8,092.15
	Total	9,108.02		Total	9,108.02

VAT ACCOUNT					
Date 20X1	Reference	Debit £	Date 20X1	Reference	Credit £
31/03	PDB	1,625.49	31/03	SDB	3,097.12
31/03	SRDB	325.15	31/03	PRDB	187.09
	Bal c/d	1,333.57			
	Total	3,284.21		Total	3,284.21

Abbreviations key

SDB – sales day book, SDRB – sales returns day book

PDB – purchases day book, PRDB – purchase returns day book

Required

Prepare the VAT return for the quarter ended 31 March.

Proforma VAT return for completion

		£
VAT due in this period on **sales** and other outputs	**Box 1**	
VAT due in this period on **acquisitions** from other **EC Member States**	**Box 2**	
Total VAT due (**the sum of boxes 1 and 2**)	**Box 3**	
VAT reclaimed in the period on **purchases** and other inputs, including acquisitions from the EC	**Box 4**	
Net VAT to be paid to HM Revenue & Customs or reclaimed by you (**Difference between boxes 3 and 4**)	**Box 5**	
Total value of **sales** and all other outputs excluding any VAT. **Include your box 8 figure**	**Box 6**	
Total value of purchases and all other inputs excluding any VAT. **Include your box 9 figure**	**Box 7**	
Total value of all **supplies** of goods and related costs, excluding any VAT, to other **EC Member States**	**Box 8**	
Total value of all **acquisitions** of goods and related costs, excluding any VAT, from other **EC Member States**	**Box 9**	

2.4 VAT: Adjustment of previous errors

You will notice in the pro-forma VAT account that there are entries for net under claims and net over claims.

Net errors made in previous VAT returns which are below the disclosure threshold can be adjusted for on the VAT return through the VAT account.

The error threshold was discussed in Chapter 6.

As a reminder errors can be corrected on the next VAT return if they are:

- No more than £10,000
- Between £10,000 and £50,000 but no more than 1% of turnover for the current return period (specifically the figure included in Box 6 of the return)

An error affecting output tax is adjusted by adding or subtracting it to box 1. An error affecting input tax is adjusted for in Box 4. If there are several errors they are netted off and the one single figure for net errors will then be entered as additional input tax in Box 4 if there has been an earlier net under claim of VAT and as additional output tax in Box 1 if the net error was a net over claim in a previous return.

2.5 Errors above the threshold

The VAT office should be informed immediately either by a letter or on Form VAT 652. This is known as voluntary disclosure.

The information provided to the VAT office should be:

- how the error happened
- the amount of the error
- the VAT period in which it occurred
- whether the error was involving input or output tax
- how you worked out the error
- whether the error is in favour of the business or HMRC.

2.6 VAT: Bad debt relief

You will notice that there is an entry in the pro-forma VAT account for bad debt relief as additional input tax.

When a supplier invoices a customer for an amount including VAT, the supplier must pay the VAT to HMRC.

If the customer then fails to pay the debt, the supplier's position is that he has paid output VAT which he has never collected. This is obviously unfair, and the system allows him to recover such amounts.

Suppliers cannot issue credit notes to recover VAT on bad debts.

Instead, the business must make an **adjustment through the VAT return**. The business can reclaim VAT already paid over if:

- output tax was paid on the original supply
- six months have elapsed between the date payment was due (or the date of supply if later) and the date of the VAT return, and
- the debt has been written off as a bad debt in the accounting records
- the debt is less than 3 years and 6 months old
- the debt has not been sold to a factoring company
- you did not charge more than the selling price for the items.

If the business receives a **repayment of the debt later**, it must make an adjustment to the VAT relief claimed.

The bad debt relief is entered in Box 4 of the return along with the VAT on purchases.

Be very careful when computing the VAT on the bad debt.

The amount of the bad debt will be VAT inclusive, because the amount the debtor owes is the amount that includes VAT.

To calculate the VAT you have to multiply the bad debt by 20/120 (or 1/6) for the standard VAT rate of 20%.

🔆 Example

A business has made purchases of £237,000 (net of VAT) in the VAT quarter and has written off a bad debt of £750. They also have a net under claim of VAT of £1,250.00 from earlier periods.

Calculate the figure that will be entered on the VAT return for the quarter in Box 4.

Solution

	£	£ p
Purchases (net of VAT)	237,000	
VAT thereon (£237,000 × 0.20)		47,400.00
Bad debt	750	
VAT thereon (£750 × 20/120)		125.00
Net under claim of VAT		1,250.00
Total VAT for Box 4		48,775.00

Reference material

The conditions for bad debt relief are included in the official VAT reference material provided in the real assessment, so you do not need to learn them.

You need to be familiar with the location and content of the material as in the assessment you will need to access the correct part of the reference material from a series of clickable links.

Why not look up the correct part of the Official Reference Material in the Appendix to this textbook now?

3 Communicating VAT information

3.1 Advising managers of the impact of VAT payments

Once the return has been completed it must be submitted to HMRC and any VAT owing paid over to HMRC. Most businesses submit and pay electronically.

In your assessment you may be asked to complete a short email to the financial accountant or another manager, giving the details of the return submission and the amount payable or receivable.

It will be important for the financial accountant (or other person responsible for managing the business cash), to know when the payment will be made, so that they can make sure that the funds are available in the bank account at the correct time.

You may be required to complete something along the following lines:

Example

To: Financial Accountant
From: Dawn Jones
Date: 17 April 20X1
Subject: VAT return

I have completed the VAT return for the quarter ended 31 March 20X1.

The amount of VAT payable will be £23,561.42.

This will be paid electronically by 7 May 20X1.

If you need any further information please contact me.

Best wishes
Dawn (Junior Accountant)

 Summary

In this chapter the actual completion of the VAT return was considered. A business should keep a VAT account which summarises all of the VAT from the accounting records and this can be used to complete the first five boxes on the VAT return. The figure for VAT due to or from HM Revenue and Customs on the VAT return should equal the balance on the VAT account.

In order to complete the remaining boxes on the VAT return information will be required from the accounting records of the business, normally in the form of the day books.

As well as completing the VAT return you will need to be able to advise the relevant person of the payment or repayment needed.

5 Test your knowledge

 Workbook Activity 3

You are a self-employed accounting technician and Duncan Bye, a motor engineer, is one of your clients. He is registered for VAT.

His records for the quarter ended 30 June 20X1 showed the following:

Sales day book

	Gross £	Net £	VAT £
April	8,100.00	6,750.00	1,350.00
May	7,812.00	6,510.00	1,302.00
June	9,888.00	8,240.00	1,648.00
	25,800.00	21,500.00	4,300.00

Purchases day book

	Gross £	Net £	VAT £
April	3,780.00	3,150.00	630.00
May	3,924.00	3,270.00	654.00
June	3,216.00	2,680.00	536.00
	10,920.00	9,100.00	1,820.00

He also gives you some details of petty cash expenditure in the quarter.

	£ p
Net purchases	75.60
VAT	15.12
	90.72

Duncan understated his output VAT by £24 on his last return.

Prepare the following VAT form 100 for the period.

		£
VAT due in this period on **sales** and other outputs	**Box 1**	43204
VAT due in this period on **acquisitions** from other **EC Member States**	**Box 2**	0
Total VAT due (**the sum of boxes 1 and 2**)	**Box 3**	4224
VAT reclaimed in the period on **purchases** and other inputs, including acquisitions from the EC	**Box 4**	1855.12
Net VAT to be paid to HM Revenue & Customs or reclaimed by you (**Difference between boxes 3 and 4**)	**Box 5**	2488.88
Total value of **sales** and all other outputs excluding any VAT. **Include your box 8 figure**	**Box 6**	21500
Total value of purchases and all other inputs excluding any VAT. **Include your box 9 figure**	**Box 7**	9175.68
Total value of all **supplies** of goods and related costs, excluding any VAT, to other **EC Member States**	**Box 8**	0
Total value of all **acquisitions** of goods and related costs, excluding any VAT, from other **EC Member States**	**Box 9**	0

Workbook Activity 4

You are provided with the following summary of Mark Ambrose's books and other information provided by Mark for the quarter ended 30 September 20X1.

MARK AMBROSE

Summary of day books and petty cash expenditure
Quarter ended 30 September 20X1

Sales day book

	Work done	VAT	Total
	£	£	£
July	12,900.00	2,580.00	15,480.00
August	13,200.00	2,640.00	15,840.00
September	12,300.00	2,460.00	14,760.00
	38,400.00	7,680.00	46,080.00

Purchase day book

	Net	VAT	Total
	£	£	£
July	5,250.00	1,050.00	6,300.00
August	5,470.00	1,094.00	6,564.00
September	5,750.00	1,150.00	6,900.00
	16,470.00	3,294.00	19,764.00

Petty cash expenditure for quarter (VAT inclusive)

July	£108.00
August	£96.00
September	£120.00

$324 \times \dfrac{20}{120} = 54$

270

Bad debts list – 30 September 20X1

Date	Customer	Total (including VAT)
30 November 20X0	High Melton Farms	£300.00
3 January 20X1	Concorde Motors	£180.00
4 April 20X1	Bawtry Engineering	£120.00

50
30
80

These have now been written off as bad debts.

Complete boxes 1 to 9 of the VAT return for the quarter ended 30 September 20X1.

		£
VAT due in this period on **sales** and other outputs	**Box 1**	7680
VAT due in this period on **acquisitions** from other **EC Member States**	**Box 2**	0
Total VAT due (**the sum of boxes 1 and 2**)	**Box 3**	7680
VAT reclaimed in the period on **purchases** and other inputs, including acquisitions from the EC	**Box 4**	3428
Net VAT to be paid to HM Revenue & Customs or reclaimed by you (**Difference between boxes 3 and 4**)	**Box 5**	4252
Total value of **sales** and all other outputs excluding any VAT. **Include your box 8 figure**	**Box 6**	7680
Total value of purchases and all other inputs excluding any VAT. **Include your box 9 figure**	**Box 7**	8680
Total value of all **supplies** of goods and related costs, excluding any VAT, to other **EC Member States**	**Box 8**	0
Total value of all **acquisitions** of goods and related costs, excluding any VAT, from other **EC Member States**	**Box 9**	0

Overseas issues

Introduction

In the final chapter of this study text we are going to conclude our VAT studies by looking at how to deal with overseas transactions.

KNOWLEDGE

Recognise different types of inputs and outputs (1.5)

Identify how different types of supply are classified for VAT purposes (1.6)

SKILLS

Correctly identify and extract relevant data for a specific period from the accounting system (1.1)

Calculate accurately relevant inputs and outputs (1.2)

Calculate accurately the VAT due to, or from, the relevant tax authority (1.3)

Make adjustments and declarations for any errors or omissions identified in previous VAT periods (1.4)

Complete accurately and submit a VAT return within the statutory time limits along with any associated payments (1.5)

CONTENTS

1   Imports and exports
2   Acquisitions and dispatches

1 Imports and Exports

1.1 Introduction

VAT is a tax levied within the European Union (EU). It applies to sales within the EU but not to sales outside the EU (exports).

All purchases made by EU businesses are subject to VAT even if purchased from outside the EU.

The rules for dealing with purchases from outside the EU can be complex, but you only require a broad understanding of how they are dealt with.

Note that the European Union (EU) was previously known as the European Community (EC), and the VAT returns for completion in your assessment still use the old term 'EC'.

1.2 Exports and imports to or from non-EU members

(a) Generally, goods **exported** from the United Kingdom to a non-EU country are zero-rated (i.e. there is no tax charged on them, even if there normally would be) provided there is documentary evidence of the export.

As no VAT needs to be charged, there will be no output tax to include in Box 1. This is the same for all zero-rated sales.

However these export sales **are** included with other sales in Box 6 of the return.

(b) Goods that are imported from outside the EU have to have customs duty paid on them when they enter the country. Customs duty is outside the scope of Indirect Tax and is not considered further.

However, goods that would be taxed at the standard rate of VAT if supplied in the United Kingdom are also subject to VAT. The amount payable is based on their value including customs duty. This applies to **all goods** whether or not they are for business use. The aim of the charge is to treat foreign goods in the same way as home-produced goods.

The VAT is paid at the port of entry and the goods will typically not be released until it is paid. If the imported goods are for business use and the business uses them to make taxable supplies, it can reclaim the VAT paid in the usual way as input tax on the VAT return (Box 4).

The cost of the goods purchased (excluding VAT) is included with other purchases in Box 7.

Example

Meurig runs a UK VAT registered business. He imports a large amount of goods from outside the EU which would be standard rated if bought in the UK.

All the goods he sells are standard rated items. The VAT rate is 20%.

In the quarter ended 31 December 20X1 he makes sales and purchases as follows:

	£
Sales to UK businesses	70,000
Export sales outside the EU	12,400
Purchases from UK businesses	38,500
Imports from outside the EU	17,450

All these figures exclude VAT.

What are the figures to include in Boxes 1, 4, 6 and 7?

Solution

		£
Box 1	VAT on standard rated sales	
	20% × £70,000	14,000.00
Box 4	VAT on purchases	
	20% × (£38,500 + £17,450)	11,190.00
Box 6	All sales	
	(£70,000 + £12,400)	82,400
Box 7	All purchases	
	(£38,500 + £17,450)	55,950

The sales outside the EU are zero rated so there is no VAT to include in Box 1. However, UK and export sales are included in Box 6.

Imports from outside the EU are treated like normal UK purchases from the point of view of the VAT return.

2 Acquisitions and dispatches

2.1 Exports and imports to and from countries within the EU

When both the exporting and importing country are EU members, the rules differ according to whether the purchaser is a VAT registered business or not.

Note that movements of goods between EU Member States are not known as imports and exports but as **acquisitions** and **dispatches**.

In what follows we refer to HM Revenue and Customs ('HMRC') as the collecting authority, even though in different countries it will have a different name.

2.2 Sale to a VAT registered business

- When an EU member sells goods to a VAT registered business in another EU country, it is the **buyer** who pays over the VAT to HMRC (or the equivalent in the buyer's country).

- Provided the seller has the buyer's VAT number, the seller sells the goods zero rated to the buyer. The buyer will then pay VAT to HMRC at the appropriate rate. The buyer can also reclaim the VAT from HMRC.

We can summarise this as follows:

The seller

- The seller will supply the goods zero rated.

- The seller makes no entries in Boxes 1 to 4 of the VAT return (in common with other zero rated sales).

- The seller will enter the value of the sale with other sales in Box 6 **and** again in Box 8. Note the wording on the form helps you with this.

The buyer

- The VAT registered buyer will pay the seller the sale price of the goods (excluding any VAT).

- The buyer will enter the VAT output tax in Box 2 of the return and the VAT input tax in Box 4 of the return. Thus, the net amount of VAT the buyer pays to HMRC is £Nil.

- The buyer will also enter the VAT exclusive price of the goods in Box 7 (with the other purchases) and also in Box 9.

2.3 Sale to a non-VAT registered buyer

- When a sale is made to a non-VAT registered buyer, the seller has to charge VAT at the standard rate.

- The buyer will pay the VAT inclusive price to the seller.

- The entries on the return are the same as if selling to a UK customer. These sales will **not** be included in Box 8.

We can summarise this as follows:

The seller

- The seller supplies the goods and charges VAT. The seller enters the VAT in Box 1.

- The seller enters the VAT exclusive price in Box 6.

The buyer

- The non-VAT registered buyer pays the VAT inclusive price to the seller and of course makes no entries in a VAT return because he is not registered.

- Note that if a UK business has a high level of such sales to another EU country, they may have to register for VAT in that other country.

    However, this is outside the scope of this assessment.

Example

Trystan runs a UK business selling Welsh handicraft items. He has recently started to sell goods overseas. All the goods he sells are standard rated items. The VAT rate is 20%.

In the quarter ended 31 December 20X1 he makes sales as follows:

	£
Sales to UK businesses	40,000
Sales to EU registered businesses	10,500
Sales to EU non registered customers	21,000
Export sales outside the EU	12,400

All these figures exclude VAT.

What are the figures to include in Boxes 1, 6 and 8?

Solution

		£
Box 1	VAT on standard rated sales	
	20% × (£40,000 + £21,000)	12,200.00
Box 6	All sales	
	(£40,000 + £10,500 + £21,000 + £12,400)	83,900
Box 8	Sales to EC businesses	10,500

Activity 1

Bettrys runs a UK business selling standard rated pet accessories. She imports some items from overseas, both from other EU countries and from outside the EU. The VAT rate is 20%.

In the quarter ended 31 December 20X1 her purchases are as follows:

	£
Purchases from UK businesses	27,400
Purchases from EU registered businesses	13,700
Purchases from outside the EU	18,800

All these figures exclude VAT.

What are the figures to include in Boxes 2, 4, 7 and 9?

 Reference material

Much of this information is included in the official VAT reference material provided in the real assessment, so you do not need to learn it.

You need to be familiar with the location and content of the material as in the assessment you will need to access the correct part of the reference material from a series of clickable links.

Why not look up the correct part of the Official Reference Material in the Appendix to this textbook now?

2 =

4 =

7 = 59900 ✓

9 = 13700 ✓

Activity 2

The following accounts have been extracted from the business's ledgers for the quarter ended 31 August 20X0.

Sales account

Date 20X0	Ref	Debit £	Date 20X0	Ref	Credit £
31/08	Balance c/d	700,600.00	01/06 – 31/08	Sales daybook – UK sales	672,600.00
			01/06 – 31/08	Sales daybook – EU dispatches	28,000.00
	Total	700,600.00		Total	700,600.00

Purchases account

Date 20X0	Ref	Debit £	Date 20X0	Ref	Credit £
01/06 – 31/08	Purchases day book – UK purchases	230,800.00	31/08	Balance c/d	271,800.00
01/06 – 31/08	Purchases day book – imports	41,000.00			
	Total	271,800.00		Total	271,800.00

VAT account

Date 20X0	Ref	Debit £	Date 20X0	Ref	Credit £
01/06 – 31/08	Purchases daybook	40,390.00	01/06 – 31/08	Sales daybook	100,205.00

You are also told that bad debt relief of £4,200.00 is to be claimed in this quarter, and dispatches are to a VAT registered business in Germany.

Prepare the following VAT form 100 for the period.

		£
VAT due in this period on **sales** and other outputs	**Box 1**	
VAT due in this period on **acquisitions** from other **EC Member States**	**Box 2**	
Total VAT due (**the sum of boxes 1 and 2**)	**Box 3**	
VAT reclaimed in the period on **purchases** and other inputs, including acquisitions from the EC	**Box 4**	
Net VAT to be paid to HM Revenue & Customs or reclaimed by you (**Difference between boxes 3 and 4**)	**Box 5**	
Total value of **sales** and all other outputs excluding any VAT. **Include your box 8 figure**	**Box 6**	
Total value of purchases and all other inputs excluding any VAT. **Include your box 9 figure**	**Box 7**	
Total value of all **supplies** of goods and related costs, excluding any VAT, to other **EC Member States**	**Box 8**	
Total value of all **acquisitions** of goods and related costs, excluding any VAT, from other **EC Member States**	**Box 9**	

KAPLAN PUBLISHING

3 Summary

In this final chapter the rules on dealing with sales and purchases overseas have been covered.

They can be summarised as follows for a business that only makes standard rated sales and purchases:

Type of transaction	Treatment on VAT return	
Sales outside EU	Zero rated	Include sales in Box 6
Sales within EU – to VAT registered customers	Zero rated	Include sales in Box 6 and in Box 8
Sales within EU – to non VAT registered customers	Standard rated	Include VAT in Box 1 Include sales in Box 6
Purchases from outside EU	Standard rated	Include VAT in Box 4 Include purchases in Box 7
Purchases from within EU	Standard rated	Include VAT in both Box 2 and Box 4 Include purchases in both Box 7 and Box 9

Box 8 & 9 = within EU

4 Test your knowledge

Workbook Activity 3

The following accounts have been extracted from a company's ledgers

Date		Dr £	Cr £
Sales: UK			
30.6.X1	Sales day book		60,500
31.7.X1	Sales day book		89,510
31.8 X1	Sales day book		70,400
Sales: Export EU			
30.6.X1	Sales day book		15,150
31.7.X1	Sales day book		20,580
31.8 X1	Sales day book		17,890
Sales: Exports non EU			
30.6.X1	Sales day book		8,500
31.7.X1	Sales day book		7,450
31.8 X1	Sales day book		10,100
Purchases: UK			
30.6.X1	Purchases day book	34,600	
31.7.X1	Purchases day book	31,590	
31.8 X1	Purchases day book	33,670	
VAT: Output Tax			
30.6.X1	Sales day book		12,100.00
31.7.X1	Sales day book		17,902.00
31.8 X1	Sales day book		14,080.00
VAT: Input tax			
30.6.X1	Purchases day book	6,920.00	
31.7.X1	Purchases day book	6,318.00	
31.8 X1	Purchases day book	6,734.00	

Handwritten annotations: 220410, 53620, 26050, 99860, 44082, 19972

Bad debt relief on a sales invoice for £6,000 including VAT is to be claimed this quarter. *[handwritten: 1000]*

The business overstated output VAT of £2,350 in the previous quarter and this must be corrected.

Exports within the EU were to VAT registered customers.

Prepare the following VAT form 100 for the period.

		£
VAT due in this period on **sales** and other outputs	**Box 1**	47732
VAT due in this period on **acquisitions** from other EC **Member States**	**Box 2**	83620
Total VAT due (**the sum of boxes 1 and 2**)	**Box 3**	95352
VAT reclaimed in the period on **purchases** and other inputs, including acquisitions from the EC	**Box 4**	10972
Net VAT to be paid to HM Revenue & Customs or reclaimed by you (**Difference between boxes 3 and 4**)	**Box 5**	74380
Total value of **sales** and all other outputs excluding any VAT. **Include your box 8 figure**	**Box 6**	300080
Total value of purchases and all other inputs excluding any VAT. **Include your box 9 figure**	**Box 7**	71800
Total value of all **supplies** of goods and related costs, excluding any VAT, to other **EC Member States**	**Box 8**	38620
Total value of all **acquisitions** of goods and related costs, excluding any VAT, from other **EC Member States**	**Box 9**	0

Workbook Activity 4

Warhorse Ltd runs a UK business selling standard rated horse-riding accessories.

The company imports some items from overseas, both from other EU countries and from outside the EU. The VAT rate is 20%.

In the quarter ended 30 June 20X2 the details of purchases are as follows:

	£
Purchases from UK businesses	31,250
Purchases from EU registered businesses	7,650
Purchases from outside the EU	15,850

All these figures exclude VAT.

What are the figures to include in Boxes 2, 4, 7 and 9?

 Workbook Activity 5

You are required to complete a VAT return for Coleman Limited in respect of the quarter ended 31 December 20X8.

You are given the following information to assist you in this task:

1   Of the external sales of £916,000 made during the quarter ended 31 December 20X8, a total of £65,000 relates to exports to EU countries, to VAT registered customers.

The remainder of this quarter's sales was of standard rated sales to UK customers. All sales figures given exclude VAT.

2   Total purchases by the company in the quarter amounted to £310,000 of standard-rated inputs, and £23,000 of zero-rated inputs (both figures stated are exclusive of VAT).

All of these purchases were from within the UK.

3   The sales figures for October 20X8 include an invoice for standard-rated goods with a value, excluding VAT, of £3,200.

These goods were actually despatched in September 20X8 and should have been accounted for in the VAT return for the previous quarter, but were omitted in error.

4   A debt of £624, inclusive of VAT, was written off as bad during the month of December 20X8.

The related sale was made in February 20X8. Bad debt relief is now to be claimed.

Prepare the following VAT form 100 for the period.

		£
VAT due in this period on **sales** and other outputs	**Box 1**	
VAT due in this period on **acquisitions** from other **EC Member States**	**Box 2**	
Total VAT due (**the sum of boxes 1 and 2**)	**Box 3**	
VAT reclaimed in the period on **purchases** and other inputs, including acquisitions from the EC	**Box 4**	
Net VAT to be paid to HM Revenue & Customs or reclaimed by you (**Difference between boxes 3 and 4**)	**Box 5**	
Total value of **sales** and all other outputs excluding any VAT. **Include your box 8 figure**	**Box 6**	
Total value of purchases and all other inputs excluding any VAT. **Include your box 9 figure**	**Box 7**	
Total value of all **supplies** of goods and related costs, excluding any VAT, to other **EC Member States**	**Box 8**	
Total value of all **acquisitions** of goods and related costs, excluding any VAT, from other **EC Member States**	**Box 9**	

Workbook Activity 6

You are given the following summaries of the sales and purchases daybooks, the cash book and the petty cash book of Defoe Ltd.

Use this information to complete the VAT return for the quarter ended 31 March 20X8.

DEFOE LIMITED : SALES DAY BOOK SUMMARY
JANUARY TO MARCH 20X8

	JAN £	FEB £	MAR £	TOTAL £
UK: ZERO-RATED	20,091.12	22,397.00	23,018.55	65,506.67
UK: STANDARD-RATED	15,682.30	12,914.03	15,632.98	44,229.31
OTHER EU	874.12	4,992.66	5,003.82	10,870.60
VAT	3,136.46	2,582.80	3,126.59	8,845.85
TOTAL	39,784.00	42,886.49	46,781.94	129,452.43

DEFOE LIMITED : PURCHASES DAY BOOK SUMMARY
JANUARY TO MARCH 20X8

	JAN £	FEB £	MAR £	TOTAL £
PURCHASES	14,532.11	20,914.33	15,461.77	50,908.21
DISTRIBUTION EXPENSES	4,229.04	3,761.20	5,221.43	13,211.67
ADMIN EXPENSES	5,123.08	2,871.45	3,681.62	11,676.15
OTHER EXPENSES	1,231.00	1,154.99	997.65	3,383.64
VAT	4,113.67	4,639.88	4,206.98	12,960.53
TOTAL	29,228.90	33,341.85	29,569.45	92,140.20

DEFOE LIMITED : CASH BOOK SUMMARY
JANUARY TO MARCH 20X8

	JAN £	FEB £	MAR £	TOTAL £
PAYMENTS:				
TO CREDITORS	12,901.37	15,312.70	18,712.44	46,926.51
TO PETTY CASH	601.40	555.08	623.81	1,780.29
WAGES/SALARIES	5,882.18	6,017.98	6,114.31	18,014.47
TOTAL	19,384.95	21,885.76	25,450.56	66,721.27
RECEIPTS:				
VAT FROM HMRC	2,998.01			2,998.01
FROM CUSTOMERS	29,312.44	34,216.08	36,108.77	99,637.29
TOTAL	32,310.45	34,216.08	36,108.77	102,635.30

DEFOE LIMITED : PETTY CASH BOOK SUMMARY
JANUARY TO MARCH 20X8

	JAN £	FEB £	MAR £	TOTAL £
PAYMENTS:				
STATIONERY	213.85	80.12	237.58	531.55
TRAVEL	87.34	76.50	102.70	266.54
OFFICE EXPENSES	213.66	324.08	199.51	737.25
VAT	86.55	74.38	84.02	244.95
TOTAL	601.40	555.08	623.81	1,780.29
RECEIPTS:				
FROM CASH BOOK	601.40	555.08	623.81	1,780.29

Blank VAT return for completion

VAT due in this period on **sales** and other outputs	Box 1	
VAT due in this period on **acquisitions** from other **EC Member States**	Box 2	
Total VAT due (**the sum of boxes 1 and 2**)	Box 3	
VAT reclaimed in the period on **purchases** and other inputs, including acquisitions from the EC	Box 4	
Net VAT to be paid to HM Revenue & Customs or reclaimed by you (**Difference between boxes 3 and 4**)	Box 5	
Total value of **sales** and all other outputs excluding any VAT. **Include your box 8 figure**	Box 6	
Total value of purchases and all other inputs excluding any VAT. **Include your box 9 figure**	Box 7	
Total value of all **supplies** of goods and related costs, excluding any VAT, to other **EC Member States**	Box 8	
Total value of all **acquisitions** of goods and related costs, excluding any VAT, from other **EC Member States**	Box 9	

Workbook Activity 7

You are an accounting technician for a business reporting to the Financial accountant.

You have completed the following VAT return for the quarter ended 31 March 20X0

VAT return for the quarter ended 31 March 20X0		£
VAT due in this period on **sales** and other outputs	Box 1	142,371.25
VAT due in this period on **acquisitions** from other **EC Member States**	Box 2	11,340.00
Total VAT due (**the sum of boxes 1 and 2**)	Box 3	153,711.25
VAT reclaimed in the period on **purchases** and other inputs, including acquisitions from the EC	Box 4	57,785.00
Net VAT to be paid to HM Revenue & Customs or reclaimed by you (**Difference between boxes 3 and 4**)	Box 5	95,926.25
Total value of **sales** and all other outputs excluding any VAT. **Include your box 8 figure**	Box 6	859,450
Total value of purchases and all other inputs excluding any VAT. **Include your box 9 figure**	Box 7	395,000
Total value of all **supplies** of goods and related costs, excluding any VAT, to other **EC Member States**	Box 8	45,900
Total value of all **acquisitions** of goods and related costs, excluding any VAT, from other **EC Member States**	Box 9	64,800

The business does not operate any special accounting schemes.

Today's date is 20 April 20X0.

Complete this email to the financial accountant advising her of the amount of VAT that will be paid or received and the due date.

Where options are given select one.

To: **Financial accountant/accounting technician/HMRC**

From: **Financial accountant/accounting technician/HMRC**

Date: **31 March 20X0/20 April 20X0/ 30 April 20X0/7 May 20X0**

Subject :   Completed VAT return

Please be advised that I have just completed the VAT return for the quarter ended:

31 March 20X0/20 April 20X0/ 30 April 20X0/ 7 May 20X0.

The amount of VAT **receivable/payable** will be £.......................

Please arrange to pay this electronically to arrive no later than 30 April 20X0/

Please arrange to pay this electronically to arrive no later than 7 May 20X0/

Please arrange to pay this electronically to arrive no later than 31 May 20X0/

Please expect to see this as a receipt in our bank account in due course.

ANSWERS TO CHAPTER AND WORKBOOK ACTIVITIES

Answers to chapter and workbook activities

1 Chapter 1

Activity 1

1 False – VAT is an indirect tax.

2 True – VAT is charged on business transactions so the statement is correct. Jake does not need to charge VAT on the sale of his bicycle.

3 False – Businesses collect VAT on behalf of the government so this statement is incorrect.

Activity 2

1 Cannot

2 Taxable

3 Can
Cannot

Workbook Activity 3

1 False – some sales may be exempt.

2 True

3 False – zero rated supplies are taxable supplies so VAT can be recovered.

Workbook Activity 4

1   £78.75 (£472.50 x 20/120)

2   £1,050.00 (£5,250 x 20%)

3   £846.00 (£4,230 x 20%)

4   £714.00 (£4,284 x 20/120)

Workbook Activity 5

The correct answer is B.

A, C and D are all powers of HMRC.

Workbook Activity 6

The statement is false.

A taxpayer can take a case to a Tax Tribunal regardless of whether or not there has been an internal review.

Workbook Activity 7

The correct answer is C.

2 Chapter 2

 Activity 1

1   Deanna's taxable turnover will exceed £77,000 after 10 months which is at the end of March 20X1. She must notify HMRC by 30 April 20X1 and will be registered with effect from 1 May 20X1.

2   No – taxable supplies includes both standard rated and zero rated supplies.

3   Yes – traders who only make exempt supplies cannot register.

 Activity 2

Majid will exceed the registration threshold after 5 months in business, that is, at the end of February 20X1. He must notify HMRC by 30 March and will be registered from 1 April.

Jane must register under the future prospects test as her sales will immediately exceed the registration limit within the next 30 days. She must notify HMRC by 30 July and will be registered from 1 July.

Sayso Ltd cannot register as it.only makes exempt supplies.

 Activity 3

(a)   Jig Ltd must notify HMRC of their business cessation within 30 days, i.e. by 9 November 20X0. The business will be deregistered from 10 October 20X0 (date of cessation) or from a mutually agreed later date.

(b)   Eli's registration will be cancelled with effect from 1 May 20X0 (date of request) or an agreed later date.

Workbook Activity 4

1   Register now – turnover is expected to exceed the registration limit in the next 30 days.

2   Monitor and register later – turnover for the period to date does not exceed the registration limit.

3   Register now – turnover has exceeded the registration limit in the last 12 months.

4   Monitor and register later – turnover has not exceeded the limit.

Workbook Activity 5

The correct answer is B.

Two registrations are needed. One is in respect of all of Wayne's sole trader businesses, and another in respect of the partnership with his wife.

Workbook Activity 6

1   No – businesses that only make zero rated supplies can apply to be exempted from registration

2   No – if a business exceeds the registration limit it need not register if taxable turnover in the next 12 months will be below the deregistration threshold.

3   Yes – the taxable turnover of all of a trader's sole trader businesses are aggregated to determine whether the trader has exceeded the VAT threshold.

4   No – exempt supplies are not taken into account for registration.

Workbook Activity 7

1   False – if a trader fails to register when they should, then they can be asked to pay over all the output VAT they should have charged.

2   False – traders making taxable supplies can register voluntarily.

3   False – traders making only exempt supplies cannot register for VAT.

4   True – the VAT registration number must be shown on all invoices.

5   False – traders only have to deregister if they cease to make taxable supplies. If their supplies fall below the deregistration limit they can choose to deregister.

Workbook Activity 8

1   The correct answer is D.

Taxable turnover for the first 12 months to 31 December is £72,000, to 31 January £74,000, to 28 February £76,000 and to 31 March £78,000.

2   The correct answer is D

Traders must notify HMRC within 30 days of exceeding the limit.

Workbook Activity 9

The correct answer is B.

C is incorrect as the public would have to pay VAT which they could not recover. A is incorrect as it would be compulsory to complete VAT returns.

3 Chapter 3

Activity 1

1   15 July – invoice within 14 days after basic tax point (delivery date 10 July)

2   12 August – goods invoiced before delivery

3   4 September – payment received before delivery

4   13 September – delivery date

Activity 2

The correct answer is B.

	£ p
List price of goods	380.00
Less: 10% trade discount	(38.00)
	342.00
Less: 4% settlement discount	(13.68)
Amount on which VAT to be calculated	328.32
VAT (20% × £328.32)	65.66

Alternative calculation:
VAT = (£380.00 × 90% × 96%) at 20%   65.66

Activity 3

1   VAT on 6 metre hosepipes = £10.33 (£51.68 × 20% = £10.336)

2   VAT on bags of compost = £27.74 (£138.72 × 20% = £27.744)

3   VAT on kitchen units = £216.91 (£1,084.57 × 20% = £216.914)

All rounded down to the nearest penny.

Activity 4

The correct answer is D.

A purchase debit note cancels out a purchase thus reducing the purchases, or inputs, of the business and consequently reducing the input VAT of the business.

Workbook Activity 5

1   True – it is only compulsory to issue VAT invoices to registered traders.

2   False – the £250 is VAT inclusive.

3   True – VAT invoices form the evidence for the reclaim of input tax.

4   True

Workbook Activity 6

VAT must be charged on the price payable after discount.

£176.40 (£1,000 – 10% of £1,000 = £900 – 2% of £900) × 20%

£380.00 (£2,000 – 5% of £2,000) × 20%

£138.00 (£750 – 8% of £750) × 20%

Workbook Activity 7

A   1
B   2
C   3
D   1
E   3

Workbook Activity 8

A and C are false. A proforma invoice is NOT a valid tax invoice, nor is it evidence that allows the customer to reclaim input tax.

Workbook Activity 9

The correct answer is B.

A sales credit note cancels out a sale thus reducing the sales, or outputs, of the business and consequently reducing the output VAT of the business.

Workbook Activity 10

1   20 August. The invoice is raised within 14 days of the delivery date (the basic tax point) and hence a later tax point is created.

2   10 June. The issue of the proforma invoice is ignored so the receipt of payment is the tax point.

3   4 March. The invoice is raised more than 14 days after the delivery date so the tax point stays on the delivery date.

4   10 December. The goods are invoiced before delivery so this creates an earlier tax point.

Workbook Activity 11

1   The correct answer is A.
     Receipt of cash on 19 October creates a tax point

2   The correct answer is B.
     £100 is VAT inclusive so the VAT element is £16.66 (£100 × 1/6)

3   The correct answer is C.
     The goods are invoiced within 14 days of delivery so a later tax point is created.

4   The correct answer is B.
     £350 is VAT inclusive so the VAT element is £58.33 (£350 × 1/6)

Workbook Activity 12

Engineering Supplies Ltd – this invoice is a valid VAT invoice which should be processed as a March input. The input VAT of £533.46 can be reclaimed in the quarter to 31 March 20X8.

Alpha Stationery – this is a less detailed VAT invoice which should also be processed as a March input. The VAT of £2.47 (£14.84 × 20/120) can be reclaimed in the quarter to 31 March 20X8.

Jamieson and Co – this is a proforma invoice so cannot be treated as a March input. The VAT cannot be reclaimed until a valid VAT invoice is received.

Workbook Activity 13

The correct answer is C.

The invoice must show the separate rate and amount of VAT charged for each rate of VAT

The business cannot issue a simplified invoice.

4 Chapter 4

Activity 1

1   None – the car is not used 100% for business

2   £2,916.66 (£17,500.00 × 1/6)

3   £52.50 (£650.00 ÷ 2 × 1/6) VAT is recoverable on half the cost.

4   None – blocked VAT

5   £1,912.50 (£11,475.00 × 1/6) – car is used 100% for business

Activity 2

Van	£2,200.00 (£11,000 x 20%)
Car 1	£1,900.00 (£9,500 x 20%)
Car 2	Nil – this is an exempt supply because the business was not able to recover the input tax on the purchase.
Machinery	£4,200.00 (£21,000 x 20%)

 Workbook Activity 3

The correct answer is C.

A partially exempt business has to apportion input tax in proportion to the levels of taxable and exempt supplies.

However, if the exempt input tax is below the de minimis limit the whole of the input tax can be recovered.

 Workbook Activity 4

Computer	£420.00 (£2,100 × 20%)
Car	Nil – sale of a car on which the input tax was not recoverable is an exempt supply.
Van	£2,500.00 (£12,500 × 20%)
Motorcycle	£1,352.00 (£6,760 × 20%)

 Workbook Activity 5

The correct answer is C.

When a business supplies a car to an employee who uses the car at least partly privately, and pays for fuel, then the business can recover the input VAT on running costs including the fuel.

However, the company must account for output tax determined by a table of scale charges.

Workbook Activity 6

Car – No reclaim of input tax if there is some private use of the car

Overseas customer entertainment – Yes, input tax is recoverable

Staff party – Yes, input tax is recoverable

Office supplies – Yes, input tax is recoverable

Lorry – Yes, input tax is recoverable on commercial vehicles

5 Chapter 5

Activity 1

1　The correct answer is B.

　28 February 20X2 = 2 months after the year end.

2　The correct answer is A.

　Nine monthly payments must be made, each of which are 10% of the VAT liability for the previous year.

3　The balancing payment will be £580.00
　(£3,820.00 – (£360.00 × 9))

Activity 2

1　NO.　As sales are all in cash, the adoption of the cash accounting scheme would not affect the time when output tax would be accounted for but would delay the recovery of input tax until the business had paid its suppliers.

2　YES.　The business would benefit because it would only account for output VAT when the customer paid. Even though the recovery of input VAT would be delayed until the suppliers were paid, the amount of input VAT is likely to be less than output VAT so the business does gain a net cash flow advantage.

3　NO.　As the sales are zero rated no output tax is payable. The adoption of the cash accounting scheme would simply delay the recovery of input VAT until the suppliers were paid.

Activity 3

1   The correct answer is B.

£15,916.66 (20/120 × (£100,000 – £4,500))

2   The correct answer is C.

£9,000.00 (9% × £100,000)

 Workbook Activity 4

1   False – VAT invoices must still be supplied to customers.

2   False – A VAT account must still be kept.

3   True – It is possible to be in the flat rate and the annual accounting scheme.

4   False – the limit to join the scheme is £150,000.

5   True – The flat rate percentage is determined by your trade sector.

 Workbook Activity 5

1   The correct answer is D.

This is how the annual accounting scheme payments are made.

2   The correct answer is B.

31 August 20X2 – two months after the year end.

 Workbook Activity 6

1   The correct answer is C.

31 October – one month after the end of the quarter.

2   The correct answer is D.

7 November – 7 extra days are given for online submissions.

Workbook Activity 7

The correct answer is B.

VAT returns must still be completed.

Workbook Activity 8

1   False – VAT invoices must still be issued.

2   True – this is one of the advantages of the scheme.

3   False – businesses with a high level of cash sales do not benefit from cash accounting.

4   False – cash accounting does not affect customers.

5   True – this is one of the conditions for joining the scheme.

Workbook Activity 9

1   The correct answer is C.

(£80,000 – £6,100) × 20%

2   The correct answer is B.

(£80,000 + 20% of £80,000) × 8%. The percentage must be applied to the VAT inclusive figure.

Workbook Activity 10

1 The correct answer is A.

B is false as the time limit is 1 month and 7 days which can be 35, 36, 37 or 38 days depending on which month the return period ends (and whether it is a Leap year).

C is false as traders cannot pay by post if they submit electronic returns.

2 The correct answer is A.

3 The correct answer is A. (£7,200 ÷ 4) = £1,800.00

4 The correct answer is B.

5 The correct answer is A. (£75,000 × 12%) = £9,000.00

6 Chapter 6

Activity 1

1 Error £4,500.00 – include on VAT return as below £10,000

2 Error £12,000.00 – separate disclosure is needed as this error is more than £10,000 and is more than 1% of turnover

3 Error £30,000.00 – can be included on VAT return as between £10,000 and £50,000 and less than 1% of turnover

4 Error £60,000.00 – must be separately disclosed as more than £50,000

Workbook Activity 2

1   FALSE – it is the other way round. Avoidance is legal and evasion is illegal.

2   The correct answer is D.

Whether or not a penalty is charged depends on the circumstances.

3   The correct answer is B.

The error is between £10,000 and £50,000 but is more than 1% of turnover, hence it must be separately disclosed.

4   A surcharge liability notice runs for …*12*.. months after the end of the return period for which the trader is in default.

Once the surcharge period has started a VAT default occurs when VAT is paid …*late.*

A surcharge liability notice will not be issued if a trader has a …*reasonable*…excuse.

Workbook Activity 3

1   Include in VAT return. The error is less than £10,000.

2   Separate disclosure.

The error is over £10,000 and more than 1% of turnover.

3   Include in VAT return.

The error is between £10,000 and £50,000 and less than 1% of turnover.

4   Separate disclosure. The error is more than £50,000.

Workbook Activity 4

1   True

2   False – whether or not a penalty is charged depends on the circumstances.

3   False – a default occurs when a return is submitted late OR a late payment made. It does not have to be both.

4   True

7 Chapter 7

 Activity 1

Panther

A	Sales	1
B	Cash sales	7
C	Credit notes issued	2
D	Purchases	6
E	Cash purchases	7 and 9
F	Credit notes received	4
G	Capital goods sold	8 or 1 (if it is an analysed sales day book)
H	Capital goods purchased	8 or 6 (if analysed)
I	Bad debt relief	3

Activity 2

		£
VAT due in this period on sales and other outputs	Box 1	2,771.97
VAT due in this period on acquisitions from other EC Member States	Box 2	0.00
Total VAT due (the sum of boxes 1 and 2)	Box 3	2,771.97
VAT reclaimed in the period on purchases and other inputs, including acquisitions from the EC	Box 4	1,438.40
Net VAT to be paid to HM Revenue & Customs or reclaimed by you (Difference between boxes 3 and 4)	Box 5	1,333.57
Total value of sales and all other outputs excluding any VAT. Include your box 8 figure	Box 6	15,251
Total value of purchases and all other inputs excluding any VAT. Include your box 9 figure	Box 7	8,092
Total value of all supplies of goods and related costs, excluding any VAT, to other EC Member States	Box 8	0
Total value of all acquisitions of goods and related costs, excluding any VAT, from other EC Member States	Box 9	0

Workings

Box 1

	£
VAT on sales	3,097.12
Less: VAT on credit notes	(325.15)
	2,771.97

Box 4

	£
VAT on purchases	1,625.49
Less: VAT on credit notes	(187.09)
	1,438.40

Box 6

	£
Standard-rated sales	15,485.60
Zero-rated sales	1,497.56
	16,983.16
Less: Credit notes	
Standard-rated	(1,625.77)
Zero-rated	(106.59)
	15,250.80

Box 7

	£
Standard-rated purchases	8,127.45
Zero-rated purchases	980.57
	9,108.02
Less: Credit notes	
Standard-rated	(935.47)
Zero-rated	(80.40)
	8,092.15

Workbook Activity 3

		£
VAT due in this period on **sales** and other outputs	**Box 1**	4,324.00
VAT due in this period on **acquisitions** from other **EC Member States**	**Box 2**	0.00
Total VAT due (**the sum of boxes 1 and 2**)	**Box 3**	4,324.00
VAT reclaimed in the period on **purchases** and other inputs, including acquisitions from the EC	**Box 4**	1,835.12
Net VAT to be paid to HM Revenue & Customs or reclaimed by you (**Difference between boxes 3 and 4**)	**Box 5**	2,488.88
Total value of **sales** and all other outputs excluding any VAT. **Include your box 8 figure**	**Box 6**	21,500
Total value of purchases and all other inputs excluding any VAT. **Include your box 9 figure**	**Box 7**	9,176
Total value of all **supplies** of goods and related costs, excluding any VAT, to other **EC Member States**	**Box 8**	0
Total value of all **acquisitions** of goods and related costs, excluding any VAT, from other **EC Member States**	**Box 9**	0

Workings for VAT return

		£
Box 1:	From SDB	4,300.00
	Error on previous return	24.00
		4,324.00

		£
Box 4:	From PDB	1,820.00
	Petty cash	15.12
		1,835.12

		£
Box 7:	From PDB	9,100
	Petty cash (£75.60 rounded up)	76
		9,176

Workbook Activity 4

		£
VAT due in this period on **sales** and other outputs	**Box 1**	7,680.00
VAT due in this period on **acquisitions** from other **EC Member States**	**Box 2**	0.00
Total VAT due (**the sum of boxes 1 and 2**)	**Box 3**	7,680.00
VAT reclaimed in the period on **purchases** and other inputs, including acquisitions from the EC	**Box 4**	3,428.00
Net VAT to be paid to HM Revenue & Customs or reclaimed by you (**Difference between boxes 3 and 4**)	**Box 5**	4,252.00
Total value of **sales** and all other outputs excluding any VAT. **Include your box 8 figure**	**Box 6**	38,400
Total value of purchases and all other inputs excluding any VAT. **Include your box 9 figure**	**Box 7**	16,740
Total value of all **supplies** of goods and related costs, excluding any VAT, to other **EC Member States**	**Box 8**	0
Total value of all **acquisitions** of goods and related costs, excluding any VAT, from other **EC Member States**	**Box 9**	0

Workings for VAT return

		£
Box 4:	From PDB	3,294.00
	Petty cash (W1)	54.00
	Bad debts (W2)	80.00
		3,428.00

		£
Box 7:	From PDB	16,470
	Petty cash (£324 – £54) (W1)	270
		16,740

(W1)   Total petty cash expenditure = (£108 + £96 + £120) = £324

VAT on £324 = (20/120 × £324) = £54.00

(W2)   Bad debts more than six months old = (£300 + £180) = £480

VAT on £480 = (20/120 × £480) = £80

8 Chapter 8

Activity 1

Box 2	VAT on acquisitions from other EC countries 20% × £13,700	£2,740.00
Box 4	VAT reclaimed 20% × (£27,400 + £13,700 + £18,800)	£11,980.00
Box 7	Total purchases (£27,400 + £13,700 + £18,800)	£59,900
Box 9	Purchases from other EC countries	£13,700

Activity 2

VAT return
Quarter ended 31 August 20X0

		£
VAT due in this period on **sales** and other outputs	Box 1	100,205.00
VAT due in this period on **acquisitions** from other **EC Member States**	Box 2	0.00
Total VAT due (**the sum of boxes 1 and 2**)	Box 3	100,205.00
VAT reclaimed in the period on **purchases** and other inputs, including acquisitions from the EC	Box 4	44,590.00
Net VAT to be paid to HM Revenue & Customs or reclaimed by you (**Difference between boxes 3 and 4**)	Box 5	55,615.00
Total value of **sales** and all other outputs excluding any VAT. **Include your box 8 figure**	Box 6	700,600
Total value of purchases and all other inputs excluding any VAT. **Include your box 9 figure**	Box 7	271,800
Total value of all **supplies** of goods and related costs, excluding any VAT, to other **EC Member States**	Box 8	28,000
Total value of all **acquisitions** of goods and related costs, excluding any VAT, from other **EC Member States**	Box 9	0

Workings

Box 4	£
VAT on purchases from PDB	40,390.00
VAT bad debt relief	4,200.00
	44,590.00

Workbook Activity 3

		£
VAT due in this period on **sales** and other outputs	Box 1	41,732.00
VAT due in this period on **acquisitions** from other **EC Member States**	Box 2	0.00
Total VAT due (**the sum of boxes 1 and 2**)	Box 3	41,732.00
VAT reclaimed in the period on **purchases** and other inputs, including acquisitions from the EC	Box 4	20,972.00
Net VAT to be paid to HM Revenue & Customs or reclaimed by you (**Difference between boxes 3 and 4**)	Box 5	20,760.00
Total value of **sales** and all other outputs excluding any VAT. **Include your box 8 figure**	Box 6	300,080
Total value of purchases and all other inputs excluding any VAT. **Include your box 9 figure**	Box 7	99,860
Total value of all **supplies** of goods and related costs, excluding any VAT, to other **EC Member States**	Box 8	53,620
Total value of all **acquisitions** of goods and related costs, excluding any VAT, from other **EC Member States**	Box 9	0

Workings for VAT return

		£
Box 1:	From VAT account – output tax	
	(£12,100.00 + £17,902.00 + £14,080.00)	44,082.00
	Output VAT overstated	(2,350.00)
		41,732.00
Box 4:	From VAT account – input tax	
	(£6,920.00 + £6,318.00 + £6,734.00)	19,972.00
	Bad debts (£6,000 × 20/120)	1,000.00
		20,972.00
Box 6:	Sales: UK	
	(£60,500 + £89,510 + £70,400)	220,410
	Sales: Export EC	
	(£15,150 + £20,580 + £17,890)	53,620
	Sales: Export non EC	
	(£8,500 + £7,450 + £10,100)	26,050
		300,080
Box 7:	Purchases	
	(£34,600 + £31,590 + £33,670)	99,860

Workbook Activity 4

		£
Box 2	VAT on acquisitions from other EC countries	
	20% × £7,650	1,530.00
Box 4	VAT reclaimed	
	20% × (£31,250 + £7,650 + £15,850)	10,950.00
Box 7	Total purchases	
	(£31,250 + £7,650 + £15,850)	54,750
Box 9	Purchases from other EC countries	7,650

KAPLAN PUBLISHING

Workbook Activity 5

		£
VAT due in this period on **sales** and other outputs	Box 1	170,200.00
VAT due in this period on **acquisitions** from other **EC Member States**	Box 2	0.00
Total VAT due (**the sum of boxes 1 and 2**)	Box 3	170,200.00
VAT reclaimed in the period on **purchases** and other inputs, including acquisitions from the EC	Box 4	62,104.00
Net VAT to be paid to HM Revenue & Customs or reclaimed by you (**Difference between boxes 3 and 4**)	Box 5	108,096.00
Total value of **sales** and all other outputs excluding any VAT. **Include your box 8 figure**	Box 6	916,000
Total value of purchases and all other inputs excluding any VAT. **Include your box 9 figure**	Box 7	333,000
Total value of all **supplies** of goods and related costs, excluding any VAT, to other **EC Member States**	Box 8	65,000
Total value of all **acquisitions** of goods and related costs, excluding any VAT, from other **EC Member States**	Box 9	0

Workings for VAT return

		£
Box 1:	External sales	916,000
	Less: Exports to EU countries (zero rated)	(65,000)
	Standard rated sales	851,000
	Output VAT (£851,000 × 20%)	170,200.00

		£
Box 4:	VAT on standard rated purchases (£310,000 × 20%)	62,000.00
	Bad debt relief (£624 × 20/120)	104.00
		62,104.00

		£
Box 7:	Standard rated inputs	310,000
	Zero rated inputs	23,000
		333,000

Note that no adjustment is needed to the figures given in the question to calculate the numbers to be entered in the VAT return.

This is because the error does not need to be corrected by separate disclosure. The value of the error is below £10,000 so it can be corrected on this period's return.

The error is that output tax in the previous quarter was understated because a sales invoice was left out. However, the invoice has already been included in the total of outputs given in the question and hence output tax for this quarter, so does not need to be included again.

Workbook Activity 6

Defoe Ltd – VAT return for the quarter ended 31 March 20X8

		£
VAT due in this period on **sales** and other outputs	Box 1	8,845.85
VAT due in this period on **acquisitions** from other **EC Member States**	Box 2	0.00
Total VAT due (**the sum of boxes 1 and 2**)	Box 3	8,845.85
VAT reclaimed in the period on **purchases** and other inputs, including acquisitions from the EC	Box 4	13,205.48
Net VAT to be paid to HM Revenue & Customs or reclaimed by you (**Difference between boxes 3 and 4**)	Box 5	4,359.63
Total value of **sales** and all other outputs excluding any VAT. **Include your box 8 figure**	Box 6	120,607
Total value of purchases and all other inputs excluding any VAT. **Include your box 9 figure**	Box 7	80,715
Total value of all **supplies** of goods and related costs, excluding any VAT, to other **EC Member States**	Box 8	10,871
Total value of all **acquisitions** of goods and related costs, excluding any VAT, from other **EC Member States**	Box 9	0

Workings for VAT return

		£
Box 4:	From Purchase day book	12,960.53
	From Petty cash book	244.95
		13,205.48

		£
Box 6:	Total from sales day book	129,452.43
	Less: VAT included	(8,845.85)
		120,606.58

		£
Box 7:	Purchase day book total	92,140.20
	Less: VAT included	(12,960.53)
	Petty cash book total	1,780.29
	Less: VAT included	(244.95)
		80,715.01

 Workbook Activity 7

To: **Financial accountant**

From: **Accounting technician**

Date: **20 April 20X0**

Subject : Completed VAT return

Please be advised that I have just completed the VAT return for the quarter ended:

31 March 20X0

The amount of VAT **payable** will be £............95,926.25..............

Please arrange to pay this electronically to arrive no later than 7 May 20X0

MOCK ASSESSMENT

1 Mock Assessment Questions

This assessment is in TWO sections.

You must show competence in each section.

You should therefore attempt and aim to complete EVERY task in EACH section.

Each task is independent. You will not need to refer to your answers to previous tasks.

Read every task carefully to make sure you understand what is required.

Where the date is relevant, it is given in the task data.

Both minus signs and brackets can be used to indicate negative numbers UNLESS task instructions say otherwise.

You must use a full stop to indicate a decimal point.

Section 1

Task 1.1

(a) **Which two of the following statements about unregistered businesses are true?**

(i)   A business does not need to check its turnover for registration purposes until it has been trading for at least 12 months.

(ii) A business which makes a mixture of taxable and exempt supplies has to register when its taxable turnover for the last 12 months exceeds £77,000.

(iii) A business which has an annual turnover of £80,000 of reduced rate and exempt supplies can apply to be exempted from registration.

(iv) Owen runs two separate businesses each with standard rated taxable turnover of £45,000 over the last 12 months. He must register for VAT.

A   (i) and (ii)

B   (ii) and (iii)

C   (i) and (iv)

D   (ii) and (iv)

(b) **A trader who makes wholly zero rated supplies can apply to be exempt from registration.**

Choose ONE reason why the business might prefer not to be registered.

A   It makes their prices cheaper for non registered customers

B   If it has a very low level of input VAT

C   They do not have to charge VAT to customers

Task 1.2

(a) **Badella Ltd has returned some faulty goods to Lane plc and issued Lane plc with a debit note.**

What is the effect on VAT of processing this debit note in the books of Badella Ltd?

Select ONE answer.

A   Input tax will increase

B   Input tax will decrease

C   Output tax will increase

D   Output tax will decrease

(b) **A registered business supplies goods that are a mixture of standard rated, reduced rated and exempt.**

Which of the following statements is true?

Select ONE answer.

A   All the input VAT relating to standard rated goods can be reclaimed but never any relating to reduced rated and exempt supplies

B   All the input VAT relating to standard rated and reduced rated supplies can be reclaimed but never any relating to exempt supplies

C   All of the input VAT can be reclaimed

D   All of the input VAT can be reclaimed providing certain (de minimis) conditions are met

(c) **Which of the following are required to be shown on a VAT tax invoice for a UK supply?**

Tick one box for each line

	Required	Not required
Supplier's name and address		
Customer's name and address		
Customer's registration number		
Method of delivery		
Separate total of any zero rated goods included in the sale		
Any discount offered		
Delivery note number		
Total amount of VAT charged		
General terms of trade		

Task 1.3

Jacky runs a small business as a newsagent and has adopted the flat rate scheme for VAT.

In the year to 30 September 20X1 her figures for sales and purchases are as follows:

Standard rated sales (including VAT)	£69,000
Zero rated sales	£10,000
Standard rated purchases (including VAT)	£18,500

The flat rate percentage for her trade is 9%.

(a) **What is her VAT payable under the flat rate scheme?**

A   £8,416.66

B   £4,545.00

C   £7,110.00

D   £6,210.00

(b) Can Jacky also join the cash accounting scheme?

A   Yes

B   No

(c) Which of the following statements about the flat rate scheme are true?

Tick one box in each line.

	True	False
A discount of 1% is given from the flat rate percentage in the first year.		
You do not have to record how much VAT you charge on every sale in your accounts.		
You can join the scheme provided your total turnover (including exempt supplies) is below £150,000		
Using the flat rate scheme is beneficial if you make a high level of zero rated sales.		
Budgeting for cash flow is easier as you know what percentage of your turnover is payable to HMRC		

Task 1.4

(a) On which of the following vehicles, bought by registered businesses, can input VAT be reclaimed?

Tick one box on each line.

	Reclaim	No reclaim
A car bought for use by Bert, a sole trader. He plans to use the car 60% for his business and 40% privately.		
A car bought by Alana for use solely in her taxi business.		
A car bought by Sheard Ltd for general use as a pool car by all its employees		
A car bought by Bee Ltd for the sole use of its managing director who uses the car for all his business and private use.		
A van bought by Dennis for use by one of his site foremen.		

(b) **What output VAT needs to be charged on the following sales of vehicles by a VAT registered business. The rate of VAT is 20%. Calculate to the nearest pence.**

Vehicle	Sale proceeds £	Input VAT reclaimed when purchased	Output VAT £ p
Lorry	50,560	Yes	
Car	16,980	No	
Car	8,670	Yes	

(c) **Which of the following statements about reclaiming motor expenses for a registered business is true?**

Select one answer.

A   A business can reclaim all input VAT on fuel for business and private use

B   VAT on fuel for private motoring can only be reclaimed if the business keeps proper records of business and private mileage and pays the appropriate VAT fuel scale charge

C   VAT on fuel for private motoring can be reclaimed if the business pays the appropriate VAT fuel scale charge

D   A business cannot reclaim any VAT on fuel if part of it is used for private motoring

Task 1.5

(a) **A VAT registered business makes a standard rated (20%) supply of £925. A trade discount of 5% is given.**

The business offers a 2% discount if goods are paid for within 14 days and 1% if paid within 21 days. The customer pays after 27 days.

What is the correct amount of VAT to be shown on the invoice?

A   £185.00

B   £172.23

C   £175.75

D   £173.99

(b) **What is the effect of a sales credit note on the VAT return of the issuing business?**

A   Output VAT in Box 1 is reduced

B   Input VAT in Box 4 is increased

Section 2

Task 2.1

A business has the following bad debts at 31.12.20X2.

Date invoice due	Amount
	£
20.2.20X2	543.60
15.4.20X2	950.40
17.11.20X2	1,100.00

Calculate the amount of bad debt relief that can be claimed in the quarter to 31 March 20X3.

Task 2.2

The following information has been extracted from the books and records of Timms Ltd, a small company that manufactures electrical components.

Quarter to 31/12/X0	£
Standard rated sales to UK businesses	186,468
Zero rated sales to UK businesses	26,942
Standard rated sales to EC VAT registered customers	43,789
Standard rated sales to EC non registered customers	11,000
Purchases (all standard rated)	96,421
Acquisitions from EC suppliers (standard rated)	15,390

- All figures exclude VAT
- The standard rate of VAT is 20%
- Bad debt relief of £853.33 is to be claimed
- In the previous quarter the VAT on a sales invoice of £10,500 excluding VAT, for a standard rated sale to a UK customer was left out by mistake
- VAT is payable by electronic bank transfer.

Complete Boxes 1 to 9 of the VAT return for the quarter ended 31 December 20X0.

		£
VAT due in this period on **sales** and other outputs	Box 1	
VAT due in this period on **acquisitions** from other **EC Member States**	Box 2	
Total VAT due (**the sum of boxes 1 and 2**)	Box 3	
VAT reclaimed in the period on **purchases** and other inputs, including acquisitions from the EC	Box 4	
Net VAT to be paid to HM Revenue & Customs or reclaimed by you (**Difference between boxes 3 and 4**)	Box 5	
Total value of **sales** and all other outputs excluding any VAT. **Include your box 8 figure**	Box 6	
Total value of purchases and all other inputs excluding any VAT. **Include your box 9 figure**	Box 7	
Total value of all **supplies** of goods and related costs, excluding any VAT, to other **EC Member States**	Box 8	
Total value of all **acquisitions** of goods and related costs, excluding any VAT, from other **EC Member States**	Box 9	

Task 2.3

You are a junior accountant. Complete the following email to the financial accountant of Power Ltd advising of the amount of VAT that will be paid or received and the due date for the online filing of the quarterly return to 31.12.20X0.

The figure in Box 3 of the return is   £28,478.96

The figure in Box 4 of the return is   £44,999.40

Email

To:

From:

Date: 15.1.X1

Subject:

Please be advised that I have just completed the VAT return for the quarter ended (………………………).

The return must be filed by (……………………..).

The amount of VAT **(payable/receivable)** will be (£……………………………).

This will be **(paid electronically by ………………….../received directly into our bank account).**

Kind regards

---

2 Mock Assessment Answers

Section 1

Task 1.1

(a) The correct answer is D.

 (i)   is incorrect as a new business must check its turnover at the end of every month as it may reach the registration limit before the end of their first 12 months of trading.

 (iii) is incorrect as it is only a business making wholly zero rated supplies that can apply to be exempt from registration.

(b) The correct answer is B.

 As the business makes wholly zero rated supplies it would be charging VAT at 0% if it were registered.

 This has no effect on its prices and this means that A and C are incorrect.

Task 1.2

(a) The correct answer is B.

 A debit note in the books of the issuing business has the same effect as a purchase credit note. It will reduce input VAT.

(b) The correct answer is D.

(c) VAT invoice

	Required	Not required
Supplier's name and address	√	
Customer's name and address	√	
Customer's registration number		√
Method of delivery		√
Separate total of any zero rated goods included in the sale	√	
Any discount offered	√	

Delivery note number		√
Total amount of VAT charged	√	
General terms of trade		√

Task 1.3

(a) The correct answer is C.

(£69,000 + £10,000) × 9% = £7,110.00

Under the flat rate scheme the VAT payable to HMRC is calculated as a flat rate percentage of the total turnover including VAT.

(b) The correct answer is B.

A trader cannot join both the flat rate scheme and the cash accounting scheme. However, when joining the flat rate scheme it is possible to request that calculations are made on a cash basis.

(c) Flat rate scheme

	True	False
A discount of 1% is given from the flat rate percentage in the first year.	√	
You do not have to record how much VAT you charge on every sale in your accounts.	√	
You can join the scheme provided your total turnover (including exempt supplies) is below £150,000		√
Using the flat rate scheme is beneficial if you make a high level of zero rated sales.		√
Budgeting for cash flow is easier as you know what percentage of your turnover is payable to HMRC	√	

You can join the flat rate scheme provided your taxable turnover is below £150,000.

The flat rate percentage is calculated based on a typical business in that trade sector. If a business makes higher zero rated sales than typical for that sector, they will pay more VAT under the flat rate scheme.

Task 1.4

(a)   Input tax reclaim on vehicles

	Reclaim	No reclaim
A car bought for use by Bert, a sole trader. He plans to use the car 60% for his business and 40% privately.		√
A car bought by Alana for use solely in her taxi business.	√	
A car bought by Sheard Ltd for general use as a pool car by all its employees	√	
A car bought by Bee Ltd for the sole use of its managing director who uses the car for all his business and private use.		√
A van bought by Dennis for use by one of his site foremen.	√	

(b)   Output VAT on sale of vehicles

Vehicle	Sale proceeds £	Input VAT reclaimed when purchased	Output VAT £ p
Lorry	50,560	Yes	10,112.00
Car	16,980	No	None (exempt sale)
Car	8,670	Yes	1,734.00

(c)   The correct answer is C.

A business can reclaim VAT on all its fuel, both business and private, provided they pay the appropriate fuel scale charge for each vehicle.

It is not a requirement to keep proper records of the split between business and private mileage (unless only business mileage is being claimed).

Task 1.5

(a) The correct answer is B.

When a discount is offered, VAT must be calculated on the minimum price a customer could pay. It does not matter if the customer does or does not actually qualify for the discount.

	£
Value of the supply	925.00
Less: 5% trade discount	(46.25)
	878.75
Less: 2% cash discount	(17.58)
Net value for VAT	861.17
VAT at 20%	172.23
Alternative calculation:	
(£925.00 × 95% × 98%) at 20%	172.23

(b) The correct answer is A.

VAT on sales credit notes is deducted from output tax.

Section 2

Task 2.1

Bad debt relief £249.00

(£543.60 + £950.40) × 20/120 (or use 1/6) = £249.00

Task 2.2

VAT return

		£
VAT due in this period on **sales** and other outputs	Box 1	41,593.60
VAT due in this period on **acquisitions** from other **EC Member States**	Box 2	3,078.00
Total VAT due (**the sum of boxes 1 and 2**)	Box 3	44,671.60
VAT reclaimed in the period on **purchases** and other inputs, including acquisitions from the EC	Box 4	23,215.53
Net VAT to be paid to HM Revenue & Customs or reclaimed by you (**Difference between boxes 3 and 4**)	Box 5	21,456.07
Total value of **sales** and all other outputs excluding any VAT. **Include your box 8 figure**	Box 6	268,199
Total value of purchases and all other inputs excluding any VAT. **Include your box 9 figure**	Box 7	111,811
Total value of all **supplies** of goods and related costs, excluding any VAT, to other **EC Member States**	Box 8	43,789
Total value of all **acquisitions** of goods and related costs, excluding any VAT, from other **EC Member States**	Box 9	15,390

Workings

Box 1

	£
UK standard rated sales	186,468
EC standard rated sales to non registered customers	11,000
(EC sales to registered customers are zero rated)	
	197,468
VAT at 20%	39,493.60
Add: Output VAT error (£10,500 × 20%)	2,100.00
Box 1 total	41,593.60

Box 2

£15,390 × 20%	3,078.00

Box 4

Purchases (UK standard rated)	96,421
Acquisitions (EC)	15,390
Figure for Box 7	111,811
VAT at 20%	22,362.20
Add: VAT reclaimed on bad debt	853.33
	23,215.53

Box 6

UK standard rated sales	186,468
UK zero rated sales	26,942
EC sales to registered customers	43,789
EC sales to non registered customers	11,000
	268,199

Task 2.3

Email
To: Financial accountant
From: Junior accountant
Date: 15.1.X1
Subject: VAT return
Please be advised that I have just completed the VAT return for the quarter ended (.........**31.12.X0**...................).
The return must be filed by (............**7 February 20X1.....**).
The amount of VAT **(receivable)** will be **£16,520.44**
This will be **received directly into our bank account**
Kind regards

PSQLJ BEHOLF

Accounting Qualification

Indirect Tax (Level 3)
Reference material

The Association of Accounting Technicians
June 2012

Reference material for AAT assessment of Indirect Tax

Introduction

This document comprises data that you may need to consult during your Indirect Tax computer-based assessment.

The material can be consulted during the practice and live assessments through pop-up windows. It is made available here so you can familiarise yourself with the content before the test.

Do not take a print of this document into the exam room with you*.

This document may be changed to reflect periodical updates in the computer-based assessment, so please check you have the most recent version while studying.

*Unless you need a printed version as part of reasonable adjustments for particular needs, in which case you must discuss this with your tutor at least six weeks before the assessment date.

Contents

Introduction to VAT

VAT is a tax that's charged on most goods and services that VAT-registered businesses provide in the UK. It's also charged on goods and some services that are imported from countries outside the European Union (EU), and brought into the UK from other EU countries.

VAT is charged when a VAT-registered business sells to either another business or to a non-business customer. This is called output tax.

When a VAT-registered business buys goods or services for business use it can generally reclaim the VAT it has paid. This is called input tax.

Her Majesty's Revenue and Customs (HMRC) is the government department responsible for operating the VAT system. Payments of VAT collected are made by VAT-registered businesses to HMRC.

Rates of VAT

There are three rates of VAT, depending on the goods or services the business provides. The rates are
- standard – 20%. The standard-rate VAT fraction is 20/120 or 1/6
- reduced - 5%. The reduced rate VAT fraction is 5/105
- zero - 0%

There are also some goods and services that are:
- exempt from VAT
- outside the scope of VAT (outside the UK VAT system altogether)

Taxable supplies

If you sell zero-rated goods or services, they count as taxable supplies, but you don't add any VAT to your selling price because the VAT rate is 0%.

If you sell goods or services that are exempt, you don't charge any VAT and they're not taxable supplies. This means that you won't normally be able to reclaim any of the VAT on your expenses.

Generally, you can't register for VAT or reclaim the VAT on your purchases if you sell only exempt goods or services. If you sell some exempt goods or services you may not be able to reclaim the VAT on all of your purchases.

If you buy and sell only - or mainly - zero-rated goods or services you can apply to HM Revenue & Customs to be exempt from registering for VAT. This could make sense if you pay little or no VAT on your purchases.

Registration and deregistration limits

Registration threshold

If, at the end of any month, your turnover of VAT taxable goods and services (taxable turnover) supplied within the UK for the previous 12 months is more than the current registration threshold of £77,000, you must register for VAT without delay. You must also register if, at any time, you expect the value of your taxable turnover in the next 30 day period alone to go over the registration threshold.

If your trading is below the threshold for registration

If your taxable turnover hasn't crossed the registration threshold, you can still apply to register for VAT voluntarily.

Deregistration threshold

The deregistration threshold is £75,000. If your taxable turnover for the year is less than or equal to £75,000, or if you expect it to fall to £75,000 or less in the next 12 months, you can either:
- stay registered for VAT, or
- ask for your VAT registration to be cancelled

Keeping business records and VAT records

If you are registered for VAT, you must keep certain business records and VAT records.

You do not have to keep these records in a set way - just so your records:
- are complete and up to date
- allow you to work out correctly the amount of VAT you owe to HMRC or can reclaim from HMRC
- are easily accessible when HMRC visits you, eg the figures you use to fill in your VAT Return must be easy to find

Business records

Business records you need to keep include the following:
- annual accounts, including income statements
- bank statements and paying-in slips
- cash books and other account books
- orders and delivery notes
- purchase and sales books
- records of daily takings such as till rolls
- relevant business correspondence

In addition to these business records, you need to keep VAT records and a VAT account.

VAT records

In general, you must keep the following VAT records:

- Records of all the standard-rated, reduced rate, zero-rated and exempt goods and services that you buy or sell.

- Copies of all sales invoices you issue. However, if you are a retailer you do not have to keep copies of any less detailed (simplified) VAT invoices for items under £250 including VAT

- All purchase invoices for items you buy.

- All credit notes and debit notes you receive.

- Copies of all credit notes and debit notes you issue.

- Records of any goods or services bought for which you cannot reclaim the VAT, such as business entertainment.

- Records of any goods you export.

- Any adjustments, such as corrections to your accounts or amended VAT invoices.

- A VAT account

For how long must VAT records be kept?

Generally you must keep all your business records that are relevant for VAT for at least six years. If this causes you serious problems in terms of storage or costs, then HMRC may allow you to keep some records for a shorter period.

Keeping a VAT account

A VAT account is the separate record you must keep of the VAT you charged on your sales (output VAT or VAT payable) and the VAT you paid on your purchases (input VAT or VAT reclaimable). It provides the link between your business records and your VAT Return. You need to add up the VAT in your sales and purchases records and then transfer these totals to your VAT account, using separate headings for VAT payable and VAT reclaimable.

You can keep your VAT account in whatever way suits your business best, as long as it includes information about the VAT that you:

- owe on your sales
- owe on acquisitions from other European Union (EU) countries
- owe following a correction or error adjustment
- can reclaim on your business purchases
- can reclaim on acquisitions from other EU countries
- can reclaim following a correction or error adjustment
- are reclaiming via VAT bad debt relief

You must also keep records of any adjustments that you make, such as balancing payments if you use annual accounting for VAT.

You can use the information from your VAT account to complete your return at the end of each accounting period. You subtract your VAT reclaimable from your VAT payable, to give the net amount of VAT you pay to or reclaim from HMRC.

Unless you are using the cash accounting scheme, you must pay the VAT you have charged customers during the accounting period that relates to the return, even if they have not paid you.

Exempt and partly-exempt businesses

Exempt goods and services

There are some goods and services on which VAT is not charged.

Exempt supplies are not taxable for VAT. So you do not include sales of exempt goods or services in your taxable turnover for VAT purposes. If you buy exempt items, there is no VAT to reclaim.

This is different to zero-rated supplies. In both cases VAT is not added to the selling price, but zero-rated goods or services are taxable for VAT at 0%.

If you only sell or supply exempt goods or services

If you only sell or otherwise supply goods or services that are exempt from VAT then your business is an exempt business. You cannot register for VAT - so you won't be able to reclaim any VAT on your purchases.

This is in contrast to the situation if you sell or otherwise supply zero-rated goods or services, where you can reclaim the VAT on any purchases that relate to those sales. In addition, if you sell mainly or only zero-rated items, you may apply for an exemption from VAT registration, but then you can't claim back your input tax.

Reclaiming VAT in a partly exempt business

If you are registered for VAT but make some exempt supplies your business is partly exempt. Generally, you won't be able to reclaim the input VAT you've paid on purchases that relate to your exempt supplies.

If the amount of input VAT incurred relating to exempt supplies is below a minimum 'de minimus' amount, input VAT can be reclaimed in full.

If the amount of input VAT incurred relating to exempt supplies is above the 'de minimus' amount, only the part of the input VAT that related to non-exempt supplies can be reclaimed.

Tax points

The time of supply, known as the 'tax point', is the date when a transaction takes place for VAT purposes. This date is not necessarily the date the supply physically takes place.

Generally, you must pay or reclaim VAT in the VAT period (tax period) in which the time of supply occurs (usually quarterly), and use the correct rate of VAT in force on that date. This means you'll need to know the time of supply/tax point for every transaction so you can put it on the right VAT Return.

Time of supply (tax point) for goods and services

The time of supply for VAT purposes is defined as follows.
- For transactions where no VAT invoice is issued (for example, sales to customers who aren't registered for VAT), the time of supply is normally the date the supply physically takes place (as defined below).
- For transactions where there is a VAT invoice, the time of supply is normally the date the invoice is issued, even if this is before or after the date the supply physically took place (as defined below).

To issue a VAT invoice, you must send (by post, email etc) or give it to your customer for them to keep. A tax point cannot be created simply by preparing an invoice.

However there are exceptions to these rules on time of supply, detailed below.

Date the supply physically takes place

For goods, the time when the goods are considered to be supplied for VAT purposes is the date when one of the following happens.
- The supplier sends the goods to the customer.
- The customer collects the goods from the supplier.
- The goods (which are not either sent or collected) are made available for the customer to use, for example if the supplier is assembling something on the customer's premises.

For services, the date when the services are considered to be supplied for VAT purposes is the date when the service is carried out and all the work - except invoicing - is finished.

Exceptions regarding time of supply (tax point)

The above general principles for working out the time of supply do not apply in the following situations.

- For transactions where a VAT invoice is issued or payment is received in advance, the time of supply is the date the payment is received or the date the invoice is issued - whichever is the earlier.

- If the supplier receives full payment before the date when the supply takes place and no VAT invoice has yet been issued, the time of supply is the date the payment is received.

- If the supplier receives part-payment before the date when the supply takes place, the time of supply becomes the date the part-payment is received but only for the amount of the part-payment (assuming no VAT invoice has been issued before this date - in which case the time of supply is the date the invoice is issued). The time of supply for the remainder will follow the normal rules - and might fall in a different VAT period, and so have to go onto a different VAT Return.

- If the supplier issues a VAT invoice more than 14 days after the date when the supply took place, the time of supply will be the date the supply took place, and not the date the invoice is issued. However, if a supplier has genuine commercial difficulties in invoicing within 14 days of the supply taking place, they can contact HM Revenue & Customs (HMRC) to ask whether they can have permission to issue invoices later than 14 days and move the time of supply to this later date.

VAT invoices

What is a VAT invoice?

A VAT invoice shows certain VAT details of a sale or other supply of goods and services. It can be either in paper or electronic form.

A VAT-registered customer must have a valid VAT invoice from the supplier in order to claim back the VAT they have paid on the purchase for their business.

What is NOT a VAT invoice?

The following are NOT VAT invoices:
- pro-forma invoices
- invoices for only zero-rated or exempt supplies
- invoices that state 'this is not a tax invoice'
- statements
- delivery notes
- orders
- letters, emails or other correspondence

You cannot reclaim the VAT you have paid on a purchase by using these documents as proof of payment.

What a VAT invoice must show

A VAT invoice must show:
- an invoice number which is unique and follows on from the number of the previous invoice - if you spoil or cancel a serially numbered invoice, you must keep it to show to a VAT officer at your next VAT inspection
- the seller's name or trading name, and address
- the seller's VAT registration number
- the invoice date
- the time of supply or tax point if this is different from the invoice date
- the customer's name or trading name, and address
- a description sufficient to identify the goods or services supplied to the customer

For each different type of item listed on the invoice, you must show:
- the unit price or rate, excluding VAT
- the quantity of goods or the extent of the services
- the rate of VAT that applies to what's being sold
- the total amount payable, excluding VAT
- the rate of any cash or settlement discount
- the total amount of VAT charged

If you issue a VAT invoice that includes zero-rated or exempt goods or services, you must:
- show clearly that there is no VAT payable on those goods or services
- show the total of those values separately

Rounding on VAT invoices

You may round down the total VAT payable on all goods and services shown on a VAT invoice to a whole penny. You can ignore any fraction of a penny. (This concession is not available to retailers.)

Time limits for issuing VAT invoices

There is a strict time limit on issuing VAT invoices. You must normally issue a VAT invoice (to a VAT-registered customer) within 30 days of the date you supply the goods or services – or, if you were paid in advance, the date you received payment. This is so your customer can claim back the VAT on the supply, if they're entitled to.

You can't issue invoices any later without permission from HM Revenue & Customs (HMRC) except in a few limited circumstances.

You need a valid VAT invoice to reclaim VAT

Even if you are registered for VAT, you can normally only reclaim VAT on your purchases if:
* you buy an item and use it for business purposes and
* you have a valid VAT invoice for the purchase

Only VAT-registered businesses can issue valid VAT invoices. You cannot reclaim VAT on any goods or services that you buy from a business that is not VAT-registered.

fied (less detailed) VAT invoices can be issued

T invoices

ail sales and you make a taxable supply of goods or services for £250 or less including VAT,
...ustomer asks for a VAT invoice, you can issue a simplified (less detailed) VAT invoice that only
needs to show:
- the seller's name and address
- the seller's VAT registration number
- the time of supply (tax point)
- a description of the goods or services

Also, if the supply includes items at different VAT rates then for each different VAT rate, your simplified VAT
invoice must also show:
- the total price including VAT
- the VAT rate applicable to the item

Exempt supplies must not be included on a simplified VAT invoice.

If you accept credit cards, then you can create a simplified invoice by adapting the sales voucher you give
the cardholder when you make the sale. It must show the information described in the six bullets above.

You do not need to keep copies of any less detailed invoices you issue.

Pro-forma invoices

If you need to issue a sales document for goods or services you haven't supplied yet, you can issue a 'proforma' invoice or a similar document to offer goods or services to customers.

A pro-forma invoice is not a VAT invoice, and you should clearly mark it with the words "This is not a VAT
invoice".

If your potential customer accepts the goods or services you're offering them and if you actually supply them,
then you'll need to issue a VAT invoice within the appropriate time limit.

If you have been issued with a pro-forma invoice by your supplier, you can't use that to claim back VAT on
the purchase. You must obtain a VAT invoice from your supplier.

Advance payments and deposits

An advance payment, or deposit, is a proportion of the total selling price that a customer pays before you
supply them with goods or services. If you ask for an advance payment, the tax point is whichever of the
following happens first:
- the date you issue a VAT invoice for the advance payment
- the date you receive the advance payment

You include the VAT on the advance payment on the VAT Return for the period when the tax point occurs.

If the customer pays you the remaining balance before the goods are delivered or the services are
performed, another tax point is created when whichever of the following happens first:
- you issue a VAT invoice for the balance
- you receive payment of the balance

So you include the VAT on the balance on the VAT return for the period when the tax point occurs

Discounts on goods and services

If any of your goods or services are discounted, you charge VAT on the discounted price rather than the full
price.

If you make an offer to a customer such as 'we will pay your VAT', VAT is actually payable to HM Revenue & Customs (HMRC) on the amount the customer would have paid on the discounted price, not the amount they have paid at the full price.

Returned goods, credit notes, debit notes and VAT

For a buyer who has received a VAT invoice

If you have returned goods to the seller for a full or partial credit you have three options:
- you can return the invoice to your supplier and obtain a replacement invoice showing the proper amount of VAT due, if any
- you can obtain a credit note or supplementary VAT invoice from your supplier
- you can issue a debit note to your supplier

If you issue a debit note or receive a credit note, you must:
- record this in your accounting records
- on your next VAT Return, deduct the VAT on the credit or debit note from the amount of VAT you can reclaim

For a seller who has issued a VAT invoice

If you receive returned goods from a customer, you have three options:
- you can cancel and recover the original invoice, and issue a replacement showing the correct amount of any VAT due, if any
- you can issue a credit note or supplementary VAT invoice to your customer
- you can obtain a debit note from your customer

If you issue a credit note or receive a debit note, you must:
- record this in your accounting records
- on your next VAT Return, deduct the VAT on the credit or debit note from the amount of your VAT payable

Entertainment expenses

Business entertainment

Business entertainment is any form of free or subsidised entertainment or hospitality to non-employees, for example suppliers and customers. Generally you cannot reclaim input VAT on business entertainment expenses. The exception is that input VAT can be reclaimed in respect of entertaining overseas customers, but not UK or Isle of Man customers.

Employee expenses and entertainment

You can reclaim VAT on employee expenses and employee entertainment expenses if those expenses relate to travel and subsistence or where you entertain only employees.

When you entertain both employees and non-employees, you can only reclaim VAT on the proportion of the expenses that is for employees.

Vehicles and motoring expenses

VAT and vehicles

When you buy a car you generally can't reclaim the VAT. There are some exceptions - for example, when the car is used mainly as one of the following:
- a taxi
- for driving instruction
- for self-drive hire

If you couldn't reclaim the VAT on the original purchase price of a car you bought new, you won't have to charge any VAT when you sell it. This is because the sale of the car is exempt for VAT purposes. If you did reclaim the VAT when you bought the car new, you charge VAT when you come to sell it.

VAT-registered businesses can generally reclaim the VAT when they buy a commercial vehicle such as a van, lorry or tractor.

Reclaiming VAT on road fuel

If your business pays for road fuel, you can deal with the VAT charged on the fuel in one of four ways:
- Reclaim all of the VAT. You must use the fuel only for business purposes.
- Reclaim all of the VAT and pay the appropriate fuel scale charge - this is a way of accounting for output tax on fuel that your business buys but that's then used for private motoring.
- Reclaim only the VAT that relates to fuel used for business mileage. You'll need to keep detailed records of your business and private mileage.
- Don't reclaim any VAT. This can be a useful option if your mileage is low and also if you use the fuel for both business and private motoring. If you choose this option you must apply it to all vehicles including commercial vehicles.

Transactions outside the UK

Exports, despatches, supplying goods abroad: charging VAT

If you sell, supply or transfer goods out of the UK to someone in another country you may need to charge VAT on them.

Generally speaking, you can zero-rate supplies exported outside the European Union (EU, previously known as the European Community or EC), or sent to someone who's registered for VAT in another EU country, provided you follow strict rules, obtain and keep the necessary evidence, and obey all laws.

If you supply goods to another EU country these sales are technically known as despatches (or 'removals') rather than exports. The term 'exports' is reserved to describe sales to a country outside the EU.

VAT on sales to someone who is not VAT registered in another EU country

When you supply goods to someone in another EU country, and they're not registered for VAT in that country, you should normally charge VAT.

VAT on sales to someone who is VAT registered in another EU country

If you're supplying goods to someone who is registered for VAT in the destination EU country, you can zero-rate the supply for VAT purposes, provided you meet certain conditions.

VAT on exports of goods to non-EU countries

VAT is a tax charged on goods used in the European Union (EU), so if goods are exported outside the EU VAT isn't charged. You can zero-rate the supply.

Imports and purchases of goods from abroad: paying and reclaiming VAT

Generally speaking, VAT is payable on all purchases of goods that you buy from abroad at the same rate that would apply to the goods if supplied in the UK. You must tell HMRC about goods that you import and pay any VAT and duty that is due.

VAT on goods from EU countries

If you are registered for VAT in the UK and receive goods from inside the EU, these are known as acquisitions (or 'arrivals') rather than imports. You must enter the value of the acquisition in Box 9 and Box 7 of your VAT Return and account for VAT in Box 2 of your VAT return using the same rate of VAT that would apply if the goods were supplied in the UK. This VAT is known as acquisition tax. You can reclaim the VAT as if the goods were supplied in the UK by including the same figure in Box 4, subject to the normal VAT rules for reclaiming input tax.

VAT on imports of goods from non-EU countries

VAT may be charged on imports of goods that you buy from non-EU countries. You can reclaim any VAT paid on the goods you have imported as input tax.

Bad debts

When you can reclaim VAT on bad debts

You can reclaim VAT that you paid to HM Revenue & Customs and which you have not received from the customer. The conditions are that:

- the debt is more than six months old and less than three years and six months old
- you have written off the debt in your VAT account and transferred it to a separate bad debt account
- the debt has not been sold or handed to a factoring company
- you did not charge more than the normal selling price for the items

How to claim bad debt relief

If you are entitled to claim bad debt relief, you add the amount of VAT you are reclaiming to the amount of VAT you are reclaiming on your purchases (input tax) and put the total figure in Box 4 of your VAT return.

To work out how much bad debt relief you can claim on a VAT-inclusive balance, you need to apply the VAT fraction to the unpaid amount.

VAT periods, submitting returns and paying VAT

You must submit your VAT Return for transactions to the end of the relevant VAT period by the due date shown on the VAT Return. You must also pay any VAT due by the due date.

What is a VAT period?

A VAT period is the period of time over which the business records VAT transactions in the VAT account for completion of the VAT Return. The VAT period is three months (a quarter) unless the annual accounting scheme is used. The end dates of a business's four VAT periods are determined when it first registers for VAT, but it can choose to amend the dates on which its VAT periods end. This is often done to match VAT periods to accounting period ends.

Submitting VAT Returns online and paying HMRC electronically

It is mandatory for virtually all VAT-registered traders to submit their VAT Returns to HMRC using online filing, and to pay HMRC electronically.

Due dates for submitting the VAT return and paying electronically

You are responsible for calculating how much VAT you owe and for paying VAT so that the amount clears to HMRC's bank account on time. Paying on time will help you avoid having to pay a surcharge.

The normal due date for submitting each VAT Return and electronically paying HMRC any VAT that is owed is one calendar month after the end of the relevant VAT period, unless the annual accounting scheme is operated. You can find the normal due date for your return and payment on the return.

Online filing and electronic payment mean that in fact you get an extended due date of up to seven extra calendar days after the normal due date shown on your VAT Return to submit the Return and to pay HMRC so that the amount has cleared to HMRC's bank account. However you don't get those seven extra days in these exceptional cases:
- you use the VAT Annual Accounting Scheme
- you are required to make payments on account (unless you submit monthly returns)

If you pay HMRC by online Direct Debit, HMRC automatically collects payment from your bank account three bank working days after the extra seven calendar days following your normal due date.

If you do not have cleared funds in HMRC's bank account by your payment deadline you may be liable to a surcharge for late payment.

Special accounting schemes

Annual Accounting Scheme for VAT

Using standard VAT accounting, you must complete four VAT Returns each year. Any VAT due is payable quarterly, and any VAT refunds due to you are also repayable quarterly.

Using annual VAT accounting, you usually make nine interim payments at monthly intervals. You only need to complete one VAT Return at the end of the year when you either make a balancing payment or receive a balancing refund.

You can use annual accounting if your estimated taxable turnover during the next tax year is not more than £1.35 million. If you are already using annual accounting you can continue to do so until your estimated taxable turnover exceeds £1.6 million.

If you use the annual accounting scheme you may also be able to use either the cash accounting scheme or the flat rate scheme (but not both).

Benefits of annual accounting

- You only need to complete one VAT Return per year, instead of four.
- You get two months rather than one month to complete and send in your annual VAT return and pay the balance of your VAT payable.
- You can better manage your cash flow by paying a fixed amount in monthly instalments.
- You can make additional payments as and when you wish.
- You can join from the day you register for VAT, or if you are already registered.

Disadvantages of annual accounting

- If you regularly reclaim VAT, you will only get one repayment per year.
- If your turnover decreases, your interim payments may be higher than your VAT payments would be under the standard VAT accounting - you would have to wait until the end of the year to receive your refund.

Cash Accounting Scheme for VAT

Using standard VAT accounting, you pay VAT on your sales whether or not your customer has paid you. Using cash accounting, you do not need to pay VAT until your customer has paid you. If your customer never pays you, you never have to pay the VAT.

You can use cash accounting if your estimated taxable turnover during the next tax year is not more than £1.35 million.

You can continue to use cash accounting until your taxable turnover exceeds £1.6 million.

If you use the cash accounting scheme you may also be able to use the annual accounting scheme.

Benefits of cash accounting

Using cash accounting may help your cash flow, especially if your customers are slow payers. You do not need to pay VAT until you have received payment from your customers, so if a customer never pays you, you don't have to pay VAT on that bad debt as long as you continue to use the cash accounting scheme.

Disadvantages of cash accounting

Using cash accounting may affect your cash flow:
- You cannot reclaim VAT on your purchases until you have paid your suppliers. This can be a disadvantage if you buy most of your goods and services on credit.

- If you regularly reclaim more VAT than you pay, you will usually receive your repayment later under cash accounting than under standard VAT accounting, unless you pay for everything at the time of purchase.
- If you start using cash accounting when you start trading, you will not be able to reclaim VAT on most start up expenditure, such as initial stock, tools or machinery, until you have actually paid for those items.
- If you leave the cash accounting scheme you will have to account for all outstanding VAT due, including any bad debts.

Flat Rate Schemes for VAT

If your VAT-exclusive taxable turnover is less than £150,000 per year, you could simplify your VAT accounting by registering on the Flat Rate Scheme and calculating your VAT payments as a percentage of your total VAT-inclusive turnover. Although you cannot reclaim VAT on purchases - it is taken into account in calculating the flat rate percentage that applies to you - the flat rate scheme can reduce the time that you need to spend on accounting for and working out your VAT. Even though you still need to show a VAT amount on each sales invoice, you don't need to record how much VAT you charge on every sale in your accounts. Nor do you need to record the VAT you pay on every purchase.

Once on the scheme, you can continue to use it until your total income exceeds £230,000.

If you use the flat rate scheme you may also be able to use the annual accounting scheme.

Benefits of using a flat rate scheme

Using the flat rate scheme can save you time and smooth your cash flow. It offers these benefits:
- You don't have to record the VAT that you charge on every sale and purchase, as you would with standard VAT accounting. This can mean you spending less time on the books, and more time on your business. You do need to show VAT separately on your invoices, just as you do for standard VAT accounting.
- A first year discount. If you are in your first year of VAT registration you get a 1% reduction in your flat rate percentage until the day before the first anniversary you became VAT registered.
- Fewer rules to follow. You no longer have to work out what VAT on purchases you can and can't reclaim.
- Peace of mind. With less chance of mistakes, you have fewer worries about getting your VAT right.
- Certainty. You always know what percentage of your takings you will have to pay to HM Revenue & Customs.

Potential disadvantages of using a flat rate scheme

The flat rate percentages are calculated in a way that takes into account zero-rated and exempt sales. They also contain an allowance for the VAT you spend on your purchases. So the VAT Flat Rate Scheme might not be right for your business if:
- you buy mostly standard-rated items, as you cannot generally reclaim any VAT on your purchases
- you regularly receive a VAT repayment under standard VAT accounting
- you make a lot of zero-rated or exempt sales

Errors

Action you must take at the end of your VAT period

At the end of your VAT period, calculate the net value of all the errors you have found during the period that relate to returns you have already submitted - that is, add together any additional tax due to HM Revenue & Customs (HMRC), and subtract any tax you should have claimed back. Don't include any deliberate errors - these must be separately disclosed to HMRC.

What you do next depends on whether the net value of all the errors is less than or greater than the 'error correction reporting threshold' which is the greater of:
- £10,000
- 1% of the box 6 figure on your VAT Return for the period when you discover the error - subject to an upper limit of £50,000

If the net value of all the errors is less than the error reporting threshold then, if you prefer, you may correct the errors by making an adjustment on your current VAT Return (Method 1).

However, if the value of the net VAT errors discovered is above this threshold, you must report them to HMRC separately, in writing (Method 2).

How to adjust your VAT Return: Method 1

You can correct certain errors whose net value is below the error correction reporting threshold by adjusting your current VAT Return.

At the end of the VAT period when you discover the errors, adjust your VAT account of output tax due or input tax claimed by the net amount of all errors. Make sure that your VAT account shows the amount of the adjustment you make to your VAT Return.

If you discovered more than one error, use the net value of all the errors to adjust your return.

Adjust box 1 or box 4, as appropriate. For example, if you discover that you didn't account for VAT payable to HMRC of £100 on a supply that you made in the past, and also didn't account for £60 VAT reclaimable on a purchase, add £40 to your box 1 figure on your return.

How to separately report an error to HMRC: Method 2

For certain errors you must separately report to your relevant HMRC VAT Error Correction Team in writing about the mistake. The simplest way to tell them is to use Form VAT 652 "Notification of Errors in VAT Returns", which is for reporting errors on previous returns, but you don't have to use Form VAT 652 - you can simply write a letter instead.

You may, if you wish, use this method for errors of any size which are below the error reporting threshold instead of a Method 1 error correction. If you use this method you must not make adjustment for the same errors on a later VAT return.

You must always use Method 2 if the net errors exceed the error reporting threshold or if the errors made on previous returns were made deliberately.

Surcharges, penalties and assessments

Surcharges if you miss a VAT Return or VAT payment deadlines

You must submit your VAT Return and pay any VAT by the relevant due date. If HM Revenue & Customs (HMRC) receives your return or VAT payment after the due date, you are 'in default' and may have to pay a surcharge in addition to the VAT that you owe.

The first time you default, you will be sent a warning known as a 'Surcharge Liability Notice'. This tells you that if you pay late ('default') again during the following 12 months - known as your surcharge period - you may be charged a surcharge.

If you submit or pay late again during your surcharge period you may have to pay a 'default surcharge'. This is a percentage of your unpaid VAT. If you don't submit a correct return, HMRC will estimate the amount of VAT you owe and base your surcharge on that amount (known as an assessment – see below).

HMRC assessments

You have a legal obligation to submit your VAT Returns and pay any VAT you owe to HMRC by the relevant due date. If you don't submit a return, HMRC can issue an assessment which shows the amount of VAT that HMRC believes you owe, based on their best estimate.

Penalties for careless and deliberate errors

Careless and deliberate errors will be liable to a penalty, whether they are adjusted on the VAT return or separately reported.

If a person discovers an error which is neither careless nor deliberate, HMRC expects that they will take steps to correct it. If the person does not take steps to correct it, the inaccuracy will be treated as careless and a penalty will be due.

Penalties for inaccurate returns

You may be liable to a penalty if your VAT Return is inaccurate, and correcting this means tax is unpaid, understated, over-claimed or under-assessed. Telling HMRC about inaccuracies as soon as you are aware of them may reduce any penalty that is due, in some cases to zero.

Penalty for late registration

If you don't register for VAT with HM Revenue & Customs at the right time then you may be liable to a late registration penalty.

Finding out more information about VAT

Most questions can be answered by referring to the HMRC website.

VAT Helpline

If you can't find the answer to your question on the HMRC website, the quickest and easiest way is to ring the VAT Helpline where you can get most of your VAT questions answered. Before you ring, make sure you have your VAT registration number and postcode to hand. If you're not VAT registered you'll need your postcode.

What you can write to HMRC about

The VAT Helpline can answer most questions relating to VAT, but there may be times when you need to write to HMRC.

You can write to HMRC about VAT if:
- you've looked at the VAT information published by HMRC - either on the website or in printed notices and information sheets - and can't find the answer to your question
- you've already contacted the VAT Helpline and they've asked you to write
- you can show that you have real doubt about how VAT affects a particular transaction and your personal situation or business

If HMRC already publishes information that answers your question, they'll write to you and give the relevant details.

Visits by VAT officers

VAT officers are responsible for the collection of VAT for the government. They check businesses to make sure that their VAT records are up to date. They also check that amounts claimed from or paid to the government are correct. They examine VAT records, question the business owner or the person responsible for the VAT records and watch business activity.

Before a visit, HMRC will confirm the following details with you:
- the person the VAT officer wants to see
- a mutually convenient appointment date and time
- the name and contact number of the officer carrying out the visit
- which records the officer will need to see, and for which tax periods
- how long the visit is likely to take
- any matters you are unsure of, so that the officer can be better prepared to answer your queries

HMRC will confirm all the above information in writing unless the time before the visit is too short to allow it. They will almost always give you seven days notice of any visit unless you want an earlier one, for example to get your claim paid more quickly.

INDEX

KAPLAN PUBLISHING